101 ESSENTI
ON MANAGING BEHAVIC
SCHOC

GH00731453

101 ESSENTIAL LISTS SERIES

101 Essential Lists for the Early Years – Penny Tassoni

101 Essential Lists for Primary Teachers – Fred Sedgwick

101 Essential Lists for Secondary Teachers – Susan Elkin

101 Essential Lists for Teaching Assistants – Louise Burnham

101 Essential Lists for SENCOs – Kate Griffiths and Jo Haines

101 Essential Lists for Using ICT in the Classroom – George Cole

101 Essential Lists on Assessment – Tabatha Rayment

101 Essential Lists on Managing Behaviour in the Secondary School – Alex Griffiths and Pauline Stephenson

101 Essential Lists on Managing Behaviour in the Primary School – Alex Griffiths and Karen Jones

101 Essential Lists for Managing Behaviour in the Early Years – Simon Brownhill, Fiona Shelton and Clare Gratton

101 ESSENTIAL LISTS ON MANAGING BEHAVIOUR IN THE PRIMARY SCHOOL

Alex Griffiths and Karen Jones

continuum
LONDON • NEW YORK

Continuum International Publishing Group
The Tower Building   80 Maiden Lane
11 York Road   Suite 704
London   New York
SE1 7NX   NY 10038
www.continuumbooks.com

British Library Cataloguing-in-Publication Data
A catalogue record for this book is available from the British Library.

ISBN: 0–8264–8988–5 (paperback)

Library of Congress Cataloging-in-Publication Data
A catalog record for this book is available from the Library of Congress.

Typeset by YHT Ltd
Printed and bound in Great Britain by Ashford Colour Press Ltd,
Gosport, Hampshire

CONTENTS

Government Legislation

 Relevant guidance

For a number of years the Government has consulted, inquired and legislated on behaviour issues, the prime agenda being to raise standards. In 1988, a committee of inquiry was set up by the Secretary of State in response to widespread concern about the difficulties facing teachers in the area of discipline in schools. It produced the Elton Report which highlighted:

- the crucial role that parents had in shaping attitudes to good behaviour
- the importance of agreement between teachers, parents and pupils on the values that underlie good behaviour in schools
- problems related to attendance
- the importance of senior management teams formulating plans within school for promoting good behaviour.

The Warnock Committee (1978) stated that about 2% of children had special needs that would require special educational provision. It suggested that too many children were being placed in special education and transported out of their local community. This certainly applied to primary school children with behavioural difficulties.

Statutory guidance following such reports required LEAs and schools to have 'an inclusive ethos'. This meant:

- the provision of a broad and balanced curriculum for all children
- the removal of potential barriers to learning to ensure inclusive education
- the provision of appropriate learning opportunities and activities for all children.

1

The most important law dealing with special educational needs is the 1996 Education Act. This delivered the Special Educational Needs Code of Practice (SEN Code of Practice), which gives practical guidance on how to identify and assess children with special educational needs (this Code was revamped in 2001). It also stated that:

○ all early education settings, state schools and LEAs must take account of the Code when dealing with children who have special educational needs
○ health and social services must also take account of the Code when helping LEAs.

LIST 2   The SEN Code of Practice

The Code of Practice has far-reaching consequences for schools:

○ Special educational needs must be seen as a whole-school issue. All teachers, whatever their subject, need expertise in teaching *all* the children in their care.
○ Parents must be fully consulted about every aspect of their child's provision.
○ The views of the child are now recognized as being very important and must be sought wherever possible.
○ LEAs must provide a parent partnership service.
○ LEAs must give parents access to independent mediation services to sort out disagreements.
○ Each school must have a special educational needs coordinator (SENCO) who works in consultation with the class teacher.
○ There must be a staged approach to meeting special educational needs.
○ There should be a differentiated curriculum offered by the class teacher to ensure that children with low level needs are catered for.
○ Early Years Action/School Action is the stage in which the staff and SENCO try to identify and support a child's learning difficulties.
○ Early Years Action Plus/School Action Plus means that there will be outside agencies involved in advising about the child's education.
○ Schools may request a statutory assessment and parents have the right of appeal if the school's request is refused.
○ All schools have a copy of the government toolkit which helps with the effective implementation of the Code.

LIST 3 — The Government's Five Year Strategy

The Government's Five Year Strategy for Children and Learners was published in July 2004. It aims to give more autonomy to schools, and as they should know their budgets in advance preparation for responding to children's needs can be made. The Strategy encourages schools to evaluate their own performance and consider target-setting processes for pupils throughout school. Raising standards is an important part of the agenda but schools can also consider how best to offer additional activities and services during and outside school hours.

The part of the Five Year Strategy which helps support behaviour and attendance says that the Government will:

- inspect every school and ensure greater personalization and choice
- put the wishes and needs of children's services, parents and learners centre-stage
- open up services to new and different providers and introduce different ways of delivering services
- provide freedom and independence for frontline headteachers, governors and managers, with clear, simple accountabilities and more secure streamlined funding arrangements
- make a major commitment to staff development, with high-quality support and training to improve assessment, care and teaching
- develop partnerships with parents, employers, volunteers and voluntary organizations to maximize the life chances of children
- enable parents to get local one-stop support through children's centres that will provide childcare, education, health, employment and parenting support
- give the parents of children aged 0–2 years more opportunities and support to stay at home with their children if they want to
- provide a flexible system of 'educare' that joins up education and childcare and provides 12½ hours' free support per week for three- and four-year-olds before they go to school, with more choice for parents about when they use it
- develop dawn-to-dusk schools, with breakfast childcare and after-school clubs to help parents juggle their busy lives

4

○ set up children's trusts, bringing together all those who provide services for children and families in each local area and making sure that children at risk get proper care, education and protection.

The DfES's promises

To put the Government's Five Year Strategy into place, the DfES promises that:

○ every child will make the best possible progress in reading, writing and mathematics
○ high-quality teachers and support staff in the classroom will give children more tailored learning
○ there will be a wider school curriculum and the choice for every child to learn a foreign language, play music and take part in competitive sport
○ there will be closer relationships between parents and schools, with better information through a new 'school profile', and more family learning
○ schools will subscribe to an anti-bullying charter
○ schools will have clear rules and codes of conduct
○ more primary schools will work together in networks, supporting each other and challenging failure
○ the best headteachers will help to improve the rest; and poor schools will be turned around quickly or closed

These promises will have direct implications for staff and governing bodies who set the overarching principles on which the headteacher bases the formal anti-bullying and discipline policies. The Healthy School agenda, launched in 1999 to improve educational achievement, health and well-being, is also much broader than diet and nutrition and considers citizenship and community.

LIST 5   Every Child Matters

The Children's National Service Framework and The Children Act (2004) put children at the heart of the legislative framework. The Every Child Matters agenda seeks to provide a whole system of reforms of children's services, with the child at the centre. There are concerns that many children will not reach their potential unless there is a greater awareness of, and targets for, those most at risk. The aim is to create better outcomes for all young people by:

○ focusing on opportunities for all
○ narrowing the gaps in opportunity between certain parts of society
○ minimizing the effects of disadvantage which are felt early and often have lasting consequences where the disadvantaged and 'at risk' children and young people lag behind their peers
○ improving how services work together
○ focusing on prevention, rather than cure
○ paying heed to the effect of tragedies such as the Victoria Climbie case
○ increasing the support to parents and carers
○ emphasizing prevention, early identification and intervention
○ integrating and personalizing services for all children
○ focusing on children in need
○ implementing the duties of The Children Act (2004) to bring together local partners through children's trust arrangements
○ having organizations that listen and are responsive to the diverse needs of children, young people, their families and communities
○ recognizing that safeguarding children and young people from harm must be everyone's business.

Top tip: Keep up to date with national initiatives as these will affect your school's policies and practice.

Understanding Challenging Behaviour

2

LIST 6   Media reports

Challenging behaviour means different things to different people.
The media tends to interpret difficult behaviour as highly disruptive
and very common, making it hard for large numbers of children to
learn. Regular reports suggest that schools are being torn apart by
children's bad behaviour. You will have seen sensationalised reports
of:

- schools that struggle to handle the behaviour of one young child
- primary aged children who are being pushed around or upset by
  fellow pupils
- the impact of extreme behaviour on a whole school
- children with severe learning or emotional difficulties who are
  'running riot' and causing substantial upset and damage
- parents who struggle to manage their children's behaviour and
  can't even get them to school. They are then taken to court, even
  jailed, and the child continues to be a rampant pest!
- poor parenting skills that lead to the general breakdown of law
  and order in local communities
- the teachers who 'attack' troublemakers and get themselves into
  severe trouble
- bad behaviour blamed on heads, teachers and schools
- teachers leaving the profession in droves because they are so
  stressed by teaching difficult children.

LIST 7 The Behaviour and Attendance Strategy

The Government has responded to concerns raised by teachers and parents by launching a Behaviour and Attendance Strategy which is intended to:

○ reduce behavioural problems, both serious and low level
○ reduce exclusions
○ provide high-quality alternative provision for those who are excluded, or at risk of exclusion or of dropping out of the system
○ reduce truancy, tackle the root causes and improve attendance levels
○ ensure that effective mechanisms are in place for identifying and re-engaging children going missing from school
○ improve perceptions of behaviour and attendance among school staff, parents and the community at large.

What is challenging behaviour?

Challenge is a new pc word that means something is difficult and in some way not really expected. Challenging behaviour is any behaviour that:

○ interrupts learning
○ causes concern to a child
○ interferes with normal development
○ is harmful to any child or adult
○ could result in some kind of school failure
○ causes concern to teachers in particular
○ upsets the parents of other pupils
○ stops you enjoying the job
○ gets you into trouble with parents or colleagues
○ drives you nuts.

LIST 9 Examples of challenging behaviour

- ○ Talking in class
- ○ Verbal abuse
- ○ Interrupting or bothering other pupils
- ○ Teasing other pupils
- ○ Asking unnecessary questions
- ○ Not settling to work
- ○ Not using equipment properly
- ○ Not listening
- ○ Daydreaming
- ○ Failing to complete work assignments
- ○ Refusing to work
- ○ Damaging property
- ○ Arriving late after break – even a minute or two can disrupt the class
- ○ Not listening to the teacher
- ○ Not sitting in a seat
- ○ Complaining
- ○ Aggressive or inappropriate body language
- ○ Excessive talking
- ○ Threats of (or real) violence
- ○ Failing to work effectively
- ○ Preventing others from working
- ○ Being noisy
- ○ Silent insolence
- ○ Swearing
- ○ Anything that can irritate and stop the flow of a well-prepared lesson
- ○ Any behaviour which stops you working effectively and efficiently, even for a short time
- ○ Any behaviour which increases your blood pressure, drives you to alcohol or cigarettes, makes you bad tempered with your best friend or partner or generally stops you from enjoying your evening or weekend!

Common causes

Common causes of challenging behaviour from children include:

○ sheer boredom in a lesson, for whatever reason
○ the work takes too long
○ not able to do the work set
○ not being or feeling valued
○ not being or feeling able to contribute
○ not understanding what has to be done
○ seeking attention from the teacher or others
○ poor self-esteem
○ finding no reward in the situation
○ an argument with a friend at breaktime
○ a family upset
○ being picked on or bullied by others
○ the teacher is late or off sick
○ the class routine has been changed or ruined by one or more interruptions
○ excitement caused by school events such as sports day
○ a change in weather conditions (wind and snow can often induce over-excited behaviour)
○ an accident such as a spilt milk drink.

Your role in ensuring good behaviour

The word 'discipline' often conjures up images of punishment, but think of it as a means to promote learning, rather than punishment for wrongdoings. Here are some points to note about your role in applying discipline and promoting good behaviour.

○ Discipline can be imposed on children by others but can also come from within the child.

○ As educators it is important we teach children to be able to self-discipline. When children eventually leave home or go on to higher education, those who have self-discipline will be able to cope, whereas those used to imposed discipline will find everything much more difficult. The foundations of self-discipline should be laid early in school life.

○ If parents and teachers are too permissive, children can fail to develop a good work ethic. Excessive freedom is not a precursor to good learning. You will know children who, if given freedom to choose their workload, would opt for doing very little!

○ Middle ground is required between the punitive and the permissive styles of teaching, as children like to know where they stand and what to expect.

○ Consistency is the key – it is confusing to be reprimanded for something while another person receives no reprimand for the same apparent transgression.

○ Each environment has expectations and expected types of behaviour. We all like to feel safe and secure and have adapted to varying environments and different sets of rules. Think what it is like when your routine becomes disrupted – no cornflakes at breakfast, no sugar at school breaktime and woe betide anybody who gets in the way of your first caffeine fix!

○ Children vary in temperament and, like you, can be subject to a variety of emotions. Your own emotions can vary considerably within one school day.

○ Children bring their own problems to school. They may be helping to care for a parent or sibling, or be the child of an alcoholic parent or involved in a drug culture. They may have been up till the early hours watching inappropriate films, have struggled to find any appropriate clothing to wear for school or simply be used to doing what they want when they want. They might not have had breakfast!

o We must aim for peace in the classroom, both for our charges and for ourselves.

LIST 12   Your teaching skills

Challenging behaviour can partially be addressed by careful planning and constant evaluation of children's work and progress. There are several points you need to consider.

- ○ Our behaviour influences the behaviour of our pupils.
- ○ Strategies and techniques to improve our classroom management can be identified and learned.
- ○ Each of us needs to take responsibility for developing our skills.
- ○ Improved effectiveness will minimize our problems.
- ○ Over-disciplining can be counter productive.
- ○ Non-stop nit-picking or bombarding children with negative comments is doomed to failure.
- ○ It is important that a child realizes that you've noticed one positive rather than all the negatives.
- ○ Save time and energy for worthwhile causes and try to avoid situations where there is not likely to be a desirable outcome.
- ○ We should not be ruthless risk-takers who use power and threats to make children do what we want.
- ○ We should create options in case we can't reach an agreement, as this will prevent us from settling on an undesirable outcome.
- ○ In any situation we should do lots of listening, not just responding.
- ○ We should ask lots of questions, listen carefully and so build rapport and trust.
- ○ The best solutions for all may not be immediately evident. We must stay flexible and think creatively.
- ○ Once a child has been sanctioned for a behaviour then we should not refer to it again.
- ○ We should never let trivial occurrences escalate out of all proportion.
- ○ We should not make one-way concessions. If we give a little, pupils should give a little too.
- ○ If you have always started PE with dread, it is time to change your attitude. If your mind-set indicates you will have a bad day, then you most certainly will. Always be positive, even on Friday afternoon.
- ○ Our main aim should be to have a peaceful classroom.

Top tip: Never criticize the person, only the behaviour.

Policies, Rules and Responsibilities | 3

Your school behaviour policy

Every school should have a behaviour policy, so find out what yours says. The DfES website provides suggestions for drafting such a policy – see www.standards.dfes.gov.uk

All policies should be developed through discussion to encourage ownership. There should be discussion on:

○ the school ethos
○ the current effectiveness of the school and its procedures
○ how to run the school efficiently to encourage learning
○ what values and beliefs are held about behaviour
○ the need for all to keep rigidly to any policy.

As a minimum the policy should:

○ cover the routines in learning and teaching that govern the school day
○ emphasize achievement and success
○ establish shared and possibly individual rewards
○ specify clear sanctions and punishments
○ refer to bullying
○ emphasize that the school will be a safe place
○ comment on the responsibility and involvement of parents
○ take account of equal opportunity for all.

LIST 14 Making your policy work

You school behaviour policy should be:

○ reviewed regularly
○ strictly adhered to by all staff – whatever their views
○ changed when changes occur within the school
○ considered in the light of child protection issues.

If you are unhappy about any aspect of the policy then you must:

○ consult with your line manager
○ bring up the issue at staff meetings
○ encourage debate in the staffroom
○ always abide by the policy until it is changed
○ only take severe action if the policy is demonstrably wrong, e.g. discuss the issue with governors.

A policy is only as strong as its weakest link. Make sure you are not the weak link! Find out from the policy and from colleagues:

○ what training is available on behaviour management
○ what support systems are in place to deal with the more challenging behaviours
○ how the school obtains additional support, e.g. is there a directory of support services and a list of procedures for securing additional support?
○ where the staff handbook (which should be extensive and comprehensive) is kept
○ what the school's policy is with respect to teachers contacting parents
○ how a student is referred to the learning support unit
○ how a student is referred to other services, such as an educational psychologist or educational social or welfare worker.

Checklist for creating a policy

Use this checklist as an aide-memoire when designing or revisiting a whole-school behaviour and attendance policy.

- What are the principles behind the school policy?
- In what way do they apply to each and every member of the school?
- Are the aims of the school compatible with the principles of the policy?
- Do the principles relate appropriately to the school curriculum?
- In what ways does the policy promote positive learning?
- Does it promote positive but also effective teaching?
- In what ways does it encourage attendance?
- Consider everyone's role (including governors') to see if the policy promotes positive behaviour.
- How are rewards and sanctions used to encourage positive behaviour generally?
- Does the policy set high standards for behaviour?
- What support systems or facilities are available to help students who have learning, personal or family difficulties?
- What are the support and training arrangements for staff?
- How are parents supported, and how can they be given information to help them to be more effective and supportive to their children and the school?
- Is everyone, including parents, involved in producing the policy?
- What resources – financial as well as personal – are put into ensuring that the policy is effective?
- How will the policy be monitored to ensure that it remains effective?

Class rules

Every school needs a behaviour policy and every classroom should have its rules. There are six key areas for classroom rule-making:

❍ Communication
❍ Learning
❍ Movement in and around the classroom
❍ Personal problem-solving
❍ General code of conduct
❍ Safety.

Each rule that is agreed will:

❍ need to be fully discussed with the class
❍ be age appropriate for the class
❍ be presented in an appropriate way
❍ require defining as exactly as possible
❍ need to be taught and learnt in the same way as other curriculum areas
❍ need reviewing with the class during the year to make appropriate changes
❍ need to be displayed so that it can be pointed to
❍ be consistent with general school rules
❍ not upset colleagues, your headteacher or parents
❍ meet the needs and demands of your classroom.

It is not usually a good idea to hold in-depth discussions about sanctions for breaking the rules. Children can devise wicked punishments you cannot possibly use!

L I S T 17   Implementing the rules

Frequent rule-breaking is avoided by frequent discussions about rules, so:

- Keep the emphasis on positive behaviour.
- Start as you mean to go on – work on rules at the beginning of the term.
- Keep the list clear.
- Keep the list brief.
- Make the rules as user-friendly as you can.
- Emphasize rewards.
- Put 'In our classroom' before each rule to personalize it.
- Put your name in the list to make it more personal.
- Include any special rules.
- Ensure that there is no 'rule-bending'.
- Ask questions rather than simply repeat the rules.
- Make sure that any routines are practised.
- Do dry runs for occasional events, such as fire practice.
- If you have had any difficulty, mention the rules at the beginning of the day.
- Praise and sanction any good examples of behaviour and infringements.

LIST 18 Examples of class rules

Here are some examples of possible rules in each of the key areas (see List 16 Class rules):

Communication

- ○ We will talk quietly when we are working.
- ○ When we wish to ask questions we will put up our hand and wait our turn.
- ○ We will never talk when the teacher is talking.
- ○ We will use kind language.
- ○ We will allow and help everyone to learn.
- ○ We will respect the right of our teacher to teach.
- ○ When learning we will need to work quietly, help others and share equipment.
- ○ We will respect other people's opinions.
- ○ We will listen to instructions.

Movement

- ○ When we have to get out of our chair we will ask our teacher by putting our hand up and waiting for permission.
- ○ We will ask permission to get out of our seat only if it is really necessary.
- ○ If we get out of our seat, we will move quietly and try not to disturb others.

Personal problem-solving

- ○ When we have a problem with another person we will try and sort it out quickly and quietly on our own.
- ○ If we cannot settle our problems like this we will ask the teacher for help.
- ○ We will settle our problems without the use of verbal or physical abuse or aggression.

Treatment – code of conduct

- ○ We will try to treat everyone fairly.
- ○ We will not comment on looks or clothes.

○ We will respect each other's homes, religions and countries of birth.
○ We will keep our hands, feet and possessions to ourselves.

Safety

○ We will walk, not run, around our classroom.
○ We will look after, and return, all equipment.

L I S T 19 Essential teaching practice

It should go without saying that poor behaviour can be avoided by doing all those things that a good teacher should do. So:

- Plan, prepare and organize well.
- Have accepted classroom routines, rules and regulations and stick to them.
- Organize yourself and the materials in your classroom.
- Look at seating arrangements.
- Ensure that work is differentiated and the content appropriate.
- Keep the self-esteem of pupils high.
- Be first into the classroom.
- Look authoritative by standing in a central position.
- Give lots of eye contact.
- Thwart any trouble by acting quickly in a low-level way, e.g. using eye contact or moving closer.
- Use names and define the unwanted behaviour and the required behaviour.
- Make corrective statements short, and move on.
- Be a good role model.
- Seek help from others if you need it.
- Accept you are not perfect and that things can go wrong for you!

Top tip: Really work on your school and class rules.

Encouraging Good Behaviour 4

LIST 20   Happy pupils

Primary age children may live in difficult circumstances but we must improve the quality of their lives and learning experiences if we are to help them achieve their potential in society. Primary school is where it may start. Many of us can remember a primary teacher who had a profound influence on our lives – and wouldn't it be nice to be remembered as 'that special teacher'?

Good preparation will pay dividends in the long term. Your pupils are more likely to succeed and be happy in school if they:

○ feel valued and respected by staff and peers
○ are treated fairly
○ feel safe and secure
○ see consistency at work in school at every level
○ experience strategies that make learning interesting and dynamic
○ feel that the work is set at the right level for each of them
○ have the chance to participate in a peer mediation or conflict resolution programme in school
○ have the opportunity to use peer-support or pupil-mentorship schemes in school
○ have opportunities for learning outside the formal setting of the classroom
○ are provided with high standards of teaching and learning.

LIST 21 Being aware

It is important to be aware that children behave differently in different situations. Sometimes we focus on the bad behaviours, such as:

- not following an instruction
- attention-seeking
- being overly competitive
- getting frustrated
- being cross when failing
- persisting at a task when asked to stop
- being jealous of others
- using bad language
- not sharing or turn-taking.

Remember that a child may have faced difficult circumstances, so:

- try to make sure that parents inform you if a child has had a bad night's sleep or has been upset by something at home
- help the child to make a fresh start simply by welcoming them in a positive way, such as:
  - using the child's name
  - smiling
  - offering to help with his/her coat
  - reminding them of some fun activities which will go on during the day
  - pointing out other children who are playing happily
  - inviting them to go and join the others
  - reminding them of something that they did really well the day before.

Promoting good behaviour

Consider some of these things you could do in your classroom to encourage good behaviour.

○ Define the good behaviour you require – have clear guidelines.
○ Define bad behaviour, with reasons if necessary.
○ Display classroom rules and school rules.
○ Remind children frequently of the rules.
○ Follow agreed procedures consistently.
○ Encourage a calm and quiet atmosphere.
○ Foster a work ethic in your class.
○ Look at class size and composition (if you have any control over this) and its relevance to behaviour.
○ Consider having no-go zones in your classroom, especially in dangerous areas, bearing age in mind.
○ Group children carefully.
○ Make sure your class is presented as well as possible.
○ Use distraction as a management tool.
○ Always set achievable targets.
○ Use negotiation rather than authoritarian approaches.
○ Deflect difficult situations gently as soon as you see them coming.
○ Try always to reinforce good behaviour.
○ Record positive and negative incidents.
○ Always criticize the behaviour, never the person – whatever you feel.
○ Use an agreed reward system and supplement this if it is helpful.
○ Ensure sanctions are understood, meaningful and not rewarding.
○ Use privileges to encourage good behaviour.
○ Use very public and/or private praise regularly and often, but make sure it is not patronizing to the child.
○ Praise/reward individual acts.
○ Praise/reward group or class acts.
○ Use photographs to promote self-esteem.
○ Encourage children to report the positive actions of others.
○ Continually analyze your class management and be prepared to make changes.

L I S T 23   Keeping the peace

Here are some more strategies for ensuring positive behaviour in your school.

- ○ Be seen as fair and always keep an open mind.
- ○ Listen carefully to children before taking action – if necessary ensure that you have both 'calmed down'.
- ○ Listen carefully to parents and give them time to tell their side of the story – if they have their chance to talk they are more likely to listen carefully to you.
- ○ Contact home by telephone or letter when giving positive as well as negative messages. Follow up negative communications by positive ones (a real and regular complaint of parents).
- ○ Make sure that parents know the rules and the reasoning behind them and involve parents generally.
- ○ Use parent–teacher association (PTA) meetings to discuss positive approaches.
- ○ Become involved in organizing learning events with parents to model good relationships.
- ○ Lay on lunchtime activities to reduce opportunities for poor behaviour and organize extra-curricula activities.
- ○ If you are a senior member of staff, be seen around the school.
- ○ Be prepared to explain and discuss.
- ○ Be prepared to ask others for assistance.
- ○ If you make contracts with children, ensure that you have to give and not just take.
- ○ Follow a good marking policy.
- ○ Read the bullying policy.
- ○ Read the restraint policy, if this is likely to be an issue.
- ○ Read the equal opportunities policy.
- ○ Move forward in a focused way, using small steps.

Top tip: Remember to consider the whole child, as behaviour may reflect external influences.

Essential Class Management

What the children expect from you

Being a confident teacher who can manage difficult behaviour starts with your personal and classroom organisation. Children will feel secure and encouraged in a classroom that has clear structure and routine. Our pupils have high expectations of us as teachers. They expect that we:

- give interesting, even exciting, lessons
- provide good explanations
- always treat them with respect
- are fair to everyone in the classroom
- are friendly and, preferably, likeable to them
- have an infallible sense of humour
- keep order in the classroom as a matter of routine
- dress appropriately
- run good end-of-term events
- ensure that they don't look silly at sports events
- make sure that they get their lunch on time
- keep them safe.

To do this, our lessons should be well prepared and organized and we should pay attention to each phase of a lesson. There are various phases to all lessons and this applies to almost any supervised activity, including lunchbreaks.

Critical lesson points

- The entry and settling of the group
- The main lesson or activity
- Clear-up time
- Final exit.

Each phase has to be considered, and things to look at include:

- routines
- simplicity
- commonly accepted actions
- predictability for pupils
- common expectations.

LIST 25   The entry and settling phase

Getting the entry to a situation right will alleviate many difficulties. The routine for your pupils should be simple and predictable. You are then very definitely in charge of your domain. Something different every time could be a recipe for disaster!

○ Dress in a manner that conveys you care enough about your appearance to make an effort for them – be a good role model.
○ Ensure that you are in the classroom before the children.
○ If you are late, make sure you have a rule to ensure order, e.g. line up outside in an orderly way.
○ Consider the temperature of the room – it can influence behaviour. Open windows to make sure that the atmosphere is not stuffy.
○ If the pupils enter noisily, send them out again. Make them wait quietly, and line up in an orderly way. Stand silently, making eye contact with anyone talking or not conforming. Wait for quiet, then give clear, concise instructions for them to enter the room. Comment on any improved performance by the class. If there is a problem, repeat the process.
○ If there are issues, try a different seating arrangement. Look for random assignments rather than any choice on the part of the pupils. Try to ensure that there are no gaps in the middle of the classroom seating arrangement. When moving children, consider moving those at the back towards the front or middle of the classroom.

LIST 26 Successful entry techniques

Effective teachers always know what is happening in their classroom and from the moment the children enter the room they are in control. They:

○ greet pupils as they enter the classroom
○ place themselves in a central position, so demonstrating their authority
○ always wait for silence before speaking
○ issue any directions with authority
○ teach class rules systematically
○ utilize good aids to give effective explanations
○ use eye contact continually (the proverbial 'eyes in the back of the head')
○ always respond quickly to any inappropriate behaviour
○ give feedback to individuals and the class on learning and behaviour
○ keep contact with the whole class, using their eyes and body
○ have detailed accountability systems for themselves and their pupils.

So, consider your class entry techniques, including general greeting and your speed of response to any difficulty (a look will often suffice, no need for more).

LIST 27　Ensuring attention

Once you've got the children in and sat down, how can you ensure that you have their attention?

○ Make sure that the activity and the language you use matches the pupils' age and developmental level – attention is much greater when pupils fully understand what is required.

○ Give information in concise, clear sentences, and check frequently for understanding.

○ Always prepare pupils for change, e.g. say, 'We have just finished doing that chart, now we are going to do a slightly different type of chart.'

○ Keep unstructured time to a minimum as it leads to inattention.

○ Structure activities so that there is little room for error. Success or the expectation of success enhances attention.

○ If a pupil or group of pupils is struggling, provide additional information quickly, e.g. provide detail as to where to find information or on a page.

○ Publicly praise pupils who are attending to their work, and model good attention in your interactions.

○ Remember, children work at different rates, and apparent inattention may only be reflecting this. Intervention at an early stage may only lower self-esteem and sow the seed for future challenging behaviour.

○ Encourage good listening skills by structuring your instructions and indicating what might be expected of the pupil following these.

L I S T 2 8   Tips to maintain attention

○ Try to use pictures, diagrams or other visual aids to help verify and clarify the verbal instructions.

○ When using the SMART board make sure everyone gets a turn – it is good for children to have the excuse to move around, and the reward is instant.

○ When talking, monitor how quickly you are speaking. This helps to control the amount of information you are expecting the pupils to understand. Do not overwhelm them with too many directives and explanations at any one time.

○ Present new information in short, meaningful chunks.

○ Try to include materials that are attractive or fresh for pupils.

○ Use lighting to focus attention, e.g. try turning off the lights except for those which cover the area in which you are working.

○ Change your tone of voice to enhance pupil interest.

○ Develop active participation strategies to maintain auditory attention. Ask regular questions which require a verbal answer or a physical response such as a thumbs-up or thumbs-down sign.

○ Try to reduce distractions in your classroom. Strategies such as ensuring that pupils with attention problems cannot look out of the window can be very helpful. Sometimes it is useful to have these pupils sitting close to you.

L I S T 29   Dealing with attention difficulties

Some pupils find paying attention to the teacher particularly problematic. So,

○ Try to identify those children with an attention problem early in the school year. This can only increase your chances of success.

○ If a particular pupil has attention difficulties, place them with a group of attending, harder working, quiet children.

○ Allow pupils sufficient time to process fully any information you give them before asking for a response. If you feel that a child has not been paying attention to you, ask a low-level question rather than a question that is likely to confuse them. This brings them back, but avoids any follow-up behavioural difficulty.

○ Ensure that you are close to a pupil when giving specific personal directions or instructions – this always aids attention.

○ Ask the pupil to repeat your request in their own words to check that they know exactly what to do. Make sure you allow enough time for completion of the task.

○ Focus a child's attention by saying their name at the beginning of the request.

○ Prompt a child to pay attention to you. You could verbally request that they listen, tap them very gently on the arm, wave to get their visual attention, or put your hand on their desk.

○ Have a short 'quiet time' for the whole group and then ask a pupil to list the sounds they heard. This helps develop listening skills.

○ When giving instructions, focus on telling pupils what they can and not what they can't do.

○ Make sure there are no distracting items on the desk.

○ Have an agreement with specific individuals that a special sign, possibly known only to them, will be used to encourage attention.

○ If a pupil is working on a complex or difficult worksheet, use highlighters or outline the area of concern.

○ Use tape recorders and computers with headphones to aid concentration, listening and understanding.

○ Try to use language such as 'What are you supposed to be doing?', 'How are you getting on?', 'Are you nearing the end of the first part of this?' This can encourage concentration on the task at hand.

○ Consider having a quiet table, which children can choose to work on.

L I S T 30   The lesson

Many difficulties faced by a teacher during the lesson can be avoided by employing some simple strategies.

○ Outline the general lesson plan to the pupils, thus making the future more predictable.

○ Ensure that everything is ready, so mischief-makers don't have the time and space to make mischief.

○ Use names frequently – if you are standing in for someone else make sure you learn the children's names as quickly as possible.

○ Give praise liberally and be courteous, but do it honestly.

○ Plan and prepare the tasks, including special tasks for particular pupils.

○ Be specific about tasks new to the class.

○ Move around the classroom while the children are working, refer to them by name, and comment positively on their work. Let them observe that you are interested in them as people and in the work that they are doing, that you are monitoring how much work they are doing. Regularly encourage them to do a little more.

○ Don't interrupt an individual's work. While working they are not causing trouble. When they stop, praise them for the work they have done and move them on to the next task. This will help develop a work ethos.

○ Resolve issues as quickly and fairly as possible.

LIST 31 Responding to interruptions

Respond quickly to any interruptions, no matter how minor.

○ Give an old-fashioned authoritative stare – we all know this one and we all do it slightly differently. Develop yours and let it become your feature of disapproval, but try not to overdo it as you will soon be mimicked.

○ Ask a low-key question, so you don't put anyone on the spot. This brings attention back to the subject and away from their neighbour.

○ Use pupils' names to make comment as this personalizes the interaction and demonstrates some care on your part about them and their behaviour.

○ Use language that focuses on the behaviour not the person. Avoid 'You are naughty', use instead, 'That behaviour is not acceptable'.

○ Explain any unequal treatment to stop gossip festering. Equanimity is difficult to ensure and inequality is sometimes the best way to develop better behaviour. Explain to the group why certain sanctions or rewards have been administered and you may well find you will be given the support of the whole group

○ Talk about the effect on the curriculum and not the behaviour as this helps pupils to focus on the reasons for being in the class.

○ Loud rebukes can sometimes be effective but only if used rarely, otherwise rebuke in private. A loud noise followed by silence will gradually silence a noisy group – but allow time for the group to appreciate fully what is required. And look after your voice – it is your living.

○ An effective intervention is abrupt, short and doesn't invite further comment.

LIST 32   Clearing up and exiting

○ Maintain the structure of the lesson until the very end.

○ Determine the tasks for this time, including how you want things done, when, and who is involved.

○ Give clear, concise instructions.

○ Describe the expected behaviour as accurately as possible, e.g. 'Put the scissors away, then sit down quietly.'

○ Have a clear routine and system for dismissal. Use the last seconds to reinforce good behaviour. It is a moment of special power! They want to move on and avoid trouble elsewhere and will work together to ensure this. Don't abuse these moments, as they are brief, but give comment and praise quickly.

○ Keep the troublemaker back for a few moments only – this will be enough to disrupt his/her effect on others and disadvantages them when joining the rest of the group. And you would not want to miss your caffeine break, would you?

LIST 33 Trouble starts and finishes

Here are some simple early interventions to use at the first sign of trouble.

○ Whenever you are intervening always allow 'take-up time'. This allows pupils a little while to take in, understand and put into action your requests. Give them the opportunity to weigh up the consequences of their actions.

○ Be confident in any action you take.

○ Never be confrontational – this will always 'set you up for a fight'.

○ Never invade personal space and keep a reasonable distance at all times – no finger-wagging or face-to-face confrontations.

○ Always appear calm and look as though you are in charge, even if you don't feel it – this is the key to success.

○ Once the interaction is over, do not refer to it again unless it re-occurs shortly afterwards.

○ When interacting with your class, take up any issues as quickly as possible so that you can get on with the lesson.

○ Try 'the pause': 'Gareth (short pause), listen please. Thank you.' Try to model courtesy in all your interactions.

○ Give the pupil choice, 'Kylie, what do we do when collecting the books?' or 'Either put it away or you can give it to me.' Don't expect immediate compliance.

○ Partial agreement can help. Faced with a comment such as, 'You're not the headteacher', your reply could be, 'You're right, but I am responsible for you during lunchtime.' Or, 'William, face this way and listen please. Thanks.' 'But I'm only drawing the picture.' 'Maybe you were and now I want you to face this way and listen.'

○ State the rule, 'Jack, we have a rule for asking questions and I expect you to use it. Thanks.'

Further interventions

If you find your initial intervention is not working you will need to take further action.

○ Don't merely repeat instructions, but increase their seriousness, as in, 'Josephine, face this way, thanks', then, 'Josephine, the instruction is face this way and listen. Thank you.' And finally, 'Josephine, if you choose to ignore my instructions then you are choosing to talk to me for two minutes at breaktime.'

○ Have a quiet word, sometimes called 'conferencing'. Kneel, stoop or bend down to the pupil's level and quietly and briefly make your point. This strategy does not reduce self-esteem by making public statements; it removes the audience and therefore other potential problems, gives personal attention and makes very clear your expectation. This type of almost final intervention tends to lead to compliance.

○ Give a choice, 'If you choose not to finish your work before break then you're choosing to finish it at lunchtime. Your choice, which is it to be?' (Give take-up time before following it through.)

○ If a pupil is proving particularly difficult for you, first ensure that there really is a problem. Defining the exact behaviour that you are concerned about easily does this. All you need to do then is to count the number of times it happens in a lesson – or in a day. You may well find that the problem is not as serious as you think it is.

L I S T 3 5 Rules for interventions

○ Try to keep the flow of the lesson going wherever possible.
○ Use low-level techniques initially, such as a glance or a stare, and if in full flow, move closer to the 'offender'. Use techniques such as partial agreement to have a civilized, well-modelled interaction.
○ Try to give the pupil choices which direct them to what you want them to do.
○ Allow them take-up time to assimilate your request, make a decision and put it into operation.
○ Remember: give the instruction, remind them of this, then give a choice.
○ Don't repeat yourself but increase the 'seriousness' of your language.
○ Consider having a quiet word.
○ Be fair, consistent, polite and generally treat a pupil as you would wish to be treated, even in a problematic situation.

Top tip: Remember to act quickly and give choice and take-up time – essential for avoiding and dealing with any trouble.

Communication

6

Why communication is important

Effective communication is a symbolic system that humans have developed which sets them apart from other animals. Language is a complex code through which the rules of social interaction and appropriate behaviour are taught. From the earliest stages, children seem to be programmed to understand and respond to language and other forms of communication.

When children are very young, we communicate with them by:

○ using plenty of facial expressions and gestures
○ animating our faces to exaggerate our feelings so that children can see our expressions and gain an understanding of our emotions
○ limiting the amount of language used
○ using 'sing-song' voices
○ using very simple language, with lots of repetition
○ linking 'rough and tumble' or tactile activities to games and songs
○ developing clear routines with structures and cues.

For communication to be effective we need to:

○ provide adequate non-verbal and verbal models
○ select a subject to talk about
○ create a reason to communicate
○ be accessible to communicate with
○ make the child interested in us as a speaker
○ teach the child how to listen
○ allow the child time to respond
○ reiterate and repeat in subtly different ways
○ develop shared understanding
○ teach children the reciprocal nature of communication
○ teach good turn-taking skills.

LIST 37 Learning to communicate

Children develop their communication skills at varying rates. We need to remember that language develops differently for different children.

○ At 12 months of age some children may have a range of single words.
○ Some children do not start to use single words until they are about two years of age.
○ Children sometimes seem to spend a long time listening before they feel comfortable using single words or phrases.
○ Most children can use two- or three-word utterances by the time they are two years of age (the average adult vocabulary contains about 6,000 words).
○ Speech acquisition is slowed by hearing difficulties.

As communication is the key to all learning, when we talk to children we need to:

○ ensure that they are looking
○ check to make sure that they have heard us
○ remember that behaviour, like language, is learnt
○ repeat words using exaggerated enunciation
○ place the intonation on certain words that are important
○ repeat over and over again, e.g. songs and nursery rhymes
○ let children have the opportunity to say words that are part of a pattern
○ listen carefully to children
○ direct their attempts at communicating
○ help children quickly to develop an understanding of the timing of language, as well as the words used.

Facts about listening

Young children:

○ tend to be impulsive
○ need the opportunity to learn how to listen
○ can only concentrate on a particular topic for 1½ minutes for every year of their age
○ need to extend their concentration spans by listening
○ should have time to reflect on what has been said
○ will switch off and begin to fidget if we expect them to listen for too long
○ need help to improve listening skills. This may include playing a number of games, such as sound and picture games
○ respond very well to human voices, but may easily be distracted by events going on around them
○ often want to talk rather than listen
○ have to learn the stop–start sequence of talking and listening
○ need time to be able to respond, so that they can frame their ideas and respond appropriately
○ need to be given opportunities to hear words and language that express emotions as well as ideas and facts
○ may take time to process information and appear not to be listening even when they are thinking very hard about what has been said
○ find it very hard to concentrate when there are loud noises or complex sounds in the environment around them
○ need to know where to look so that they can listen effectively
○ may look hard at an adult's face in order to understand what is said, and the adult then feels a little unnerved by the intense attention.

You may also come across children who:

○ have suffered from hearing losses when they were young, and this may have affected their ability to listen. They can easily develop the habit of not listening if this is not encouraged and actively modelled
○ are brought up in backgrounds where nobody really listens to anybody else and yet they are expected to know how to listen when they come into school

- believe that communication is only effective when it involves shouting
- may have learnt never to respond first time to instructions
- have no skills for discussion and negotiation but know only how to demand
- are impulsive and impatient and have no understanding of other people's needs.

Learning to listen

Listening is a behaviour that, in common with many others, needs to be taught. Many young children get used to having a high level of noise around them. They may be brought up in an environment where the television is always on, and they may find it difficult to discern what they need to listen to. In many households the parental voice is often raised and angry, and children may be frightened or overwhelmed by it. In school, they need experience of positive listening activities, which encourage good attention. Here are some ideas for teaching listening skills:

o Talk very quietly.
o Use different voices for different characters in stories.
o Talk using a very high-pitched voice or very low voice, match your movements to the voice and encourage children to do the same.
o Mouth words without sounds and see if children can guess what you're trying to say.
o Hold your hand in front of your mouth and say a word quietly and see if children can recognize it, then let them have the opportunity to do the same.
o Have objects that make a noise in a box or behind a curtain so that the children cannot see them, and ask them to listen while the noise is made.
o Ask them to imitate sounds that are commonly heard and put them into a sequence of three or four sounds, e.g. a car horn, a fizzy drink being opened and a cat mewing.
o Experiment with rhyming words.
o Clap the number of syllables in words.
o Invent some nonsense words and see if the children can say them.
o Use onomatopoeic sounds such as 'splash' 'drip' 'creak' in stories and language sessions.
o Start a sentence and miss the word off the end so the children have to guess what it is.
o Tell a familiar story but add nonsense or unfamiliar words and ask the children to put up their hand when they hear these words.
o Tell a common story but change one of the facts.
o Play games such as 'I went to the shop and I bought...'

○ Give the children the opportunity to talk without interruption for a minute or two.

○ Play circle games that start the next word with the end sound of the previous word.

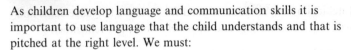

LIST 40   Using simple language

As children develop language and communication skills it is important to use language that the child understands and that is pitched at the right level. We must:

- be aware that we start to talk more quickly and include more complex instructions
- be aware that we include a wider vocabulary
- make sure that we are working at the right pace for the child
- not assume that he is 'a little adult' and can understand everything that we say
- remember that children learn best by adding small bits of knowledge to things that they already understand
- link ideas to experience
- take time to share experiences to allow vicarious learning
- be prepared to repeat the same story or song over and over again
- be prepared to spend time explaining and linking new ideas to established ones
- answer the same question over and over again (many adults are driven mad by the question 'why...?')
- be prepared to wait while a child frames a question or answer
- link the spoken language to pictures wherever possible
- remember that children have different language competencies, so make allowances for these
- try to make sure that parents are aware of the new vocabulary that is being introduced in the classroom
- provide displays and visual materials around the classroom to support discussions
- watch out for signs of children not understanding – these may include fidgeting, calling out, chatting or yawning!

Learning about language

Interaction with an adult is good for a child's language skills and will help their learning and their behaviour, but remember:

○ children may recite nursery rhymes, or part of a script from a story without knowing what particular words mean

○ children may copy phrases that they have heard an adult say, echoing what they have heard

○ adult concepts are far too difficult to understand, because they have no real meaning

○ abstract concepts, such as emotions or ones where imagination or an understanding of past and future is needed, can be very difficult for a small child to understand

○ children may use phrases in a conversation which seem to be very 'grown up' and well advanced, but in fact it is simply the child using the adult's language

○ children may be able to demonstrate perfect recall of long scripts, even though there is no understanding of the meaning

○ the language *faux pas* of children will amuse us for hours – but use them to teach about behaviour

○ children need to be reminded about the reciprocal nature of language and communication – turn-taking and giving everyone the chance to speak

○ when children are together, they may need to be taught the listen-wait-talk-wait-listen routine, to ensure that frustration levels are not raised.

LIST 42

Repetition and rules

Use repetition and rules to help children's understanding of language and behaviour. Many children find it difficult to understand or remember new concepts when they are first heard. Remember, little children are used to having messages repeated over and over again so they have time to absorb the information and store it in their long-term memory. We must not make the mistake of saying something to a small child, and in many cases to older children as well, and expect them to understand and remember it straight away. In particular, we are often using language to help change behaviour, and repetition is vital to ensure this change. We need to provide children with:

○ repetition and practice when they are learning a language
○ repetition and practice when trying to understand rules for behaviour
○ repetition and practice to understand new information about the world around them
○ access to simple language
○ access to specific language
○ language at the right level for them
○ the repetition of words and phrases
○ language supported by modelling, if necessary
○ messages delivered in a calm manner
○ opportunities to question what has been said
○ the chance to say how or why, as often as is needed
○ the chance to repeat what they have heard
○ the opportunity to pass the information on to other people – this is a good way to help a child learn
○ opportunities to develop an understanding of simple cues such as non-verbal communication – a look or a gesture is often all that is needed as a reminder
○ the chance for their parents to understand why we have particular rules in school, and why it is helpful if these are reinforced at home
○ an understanding that rules will be fairly applied throughout the school.

LIST 43 Getting the message across

It often helps to ask the child what he has been asked to do as this gives him the opportunity to verbally rehearse information. The rules we use when linking language to behaviour must be:

- simple
- fair
- applied consistently
- non-negotiable
- presented in a way that is unemotive and factual
- easily understood by the child
- within the child's competence to succeed
- designed to prevent the child becoming uncertain
- in place to help stop behaviour deteriorating
- in place to reduce the need for adults to get cross and shout
- in place to prevent the problem from being solved because everyone is cross with everyone else
- there to help prevent damage to people's self-esteem
- there to provide clear expectations which can be stated in a simple but concise way
- likely to increase our ability to implement successfully a positive behaviour approach.

Be consistent!

Consistency helps children to learn how to behave, but changing the rules without informing the child can cause confusion. We may have a rule that says, 'We all go out at playtime'. One day, because we need some help in the classroom we say to the child, 'It's okay if you stay in today', so we should not be surprised if the following day the child does not want to go out to play. We may than have to spend time explaining why the previous day was an exception. So remember,

❍ Such problems are caused by the adult not the child.
❍ It is often the child who gets into trouble for trying to bend the rules!
❍ Many children find it difficult to understand the situation if changes are made. Alternatively, many children are brought up with a high level of inconsistencies and if a teacher changes, this will be consistent with the child's expectations and the child may then continue to expect more changes.
❍ Changes to pattern and routine can cause anxiety and uncertainty. This has a knock-on effect on behaviour.
❍ Children may 'test' an adult to see if they will change other rules.
❍ Many children can be extremely persistent and ask the same question over and over again, in order to get their own way. This can be very annoying to teachers, who then become cross. It is easy to forget that the child has anticipated change and assumes that, simply by asking, it will take place.
❍ Many children are used to adults 'giving in' and assume that teachers will do the same. Any further changes in rules will reinforce this view, and very quickly all the children in the class will believe that they can influence the teacher's behaviour. If the child's best efforts are not successful, he may become grumpy because he has not got his own way. This in turn will affect other behaviours and may have a knock-on effect with his peers.

Of course, changes can be made in a classroom, but be sure that children:

❍ are pre-warned
❍ are given a clear explanation as to why they are happening

○ know what behaviours are required in the light of the changes.

At certain times of the year, e.g. Christmas, the routines are continually being disrupted and teachers may feel that many of the normal rules 'go out of the window'. When levels of disruption are at their highest, rules need to be most consistently applied to ensure that children are given reminders about how to behave. Again, it is helpful to pre-warn parents so that they know and can anticipate these and talk about them with the children.

Using specific language

As adults we use familiar, shorthand expressions which other adults understand. We may say 'be careful' when somebody is about to cross the road but we might also say that when somebody is about to cut a vegetable using a sharp knife. Such language can be confusing to a child and they may not grasp the precise meaning. Problems can arise because:

○ we believe we have delivered a message
○ we believe the child will understand and respond appropriately
○ we might become angry if the child does something else
○ the child may be cross because he/she gets it wrong.

It is much more helpful to relate language specifically to the task and to:

○ clarify statements, e.g. 'Be careful when you cross the road'
○ explain *exactly* what we want a child to do, using specific and positive language rather than general words
○ use a step-by-step approach
○ specify which rule is being used
○ avoid using a general statement, which can be meaningless or misinterpreted by the child
○ provide quick and appropriate feedback.

Some examples

○ Rather than, 'Be careful with the scissors', say, 'Hold the scissors this way' and model the correct way.
○ Rather than, 'Tidy up', say, 'Put the blocks in the box, please.'
○ Rather than, 'Be polite', say, 'Remember to say thank you.'
○ Rather than, 'Find something to do', say, 'Let's read a book or draw a picture.'

L I S T 46   The power of praise

Think of the last time somebody said 'thank you' or 'well done' to you. If you thought that the person was being genuine and really meant what they said it will have made you feel good about yourself. Praise is a powerful and important tool in behaviour management because it:

○ builds confidence
○ is very easy to give
○ costs nothing
○ helps to create a positive ethos within the classroom
○ sets a good example to others and helps to show other children correct behaviour
○ reminds us to repeat appropriate behaviour
○ helps teachers feel good about their behaviour management skills
○ increases our chances of becoming emotionally literate.

So remember:

○ children love to be praised
○ children love to hear their names – this is praise in itself (but remember also that sometimes children associate their names with a telling off!)
○ frequent praise for doing the right thing helps children to understand that by doing this, someone will notice and their name will be associated with nice words and feelings
○ you need to vary your strategy, sometimes putting the child's name at the beginning and pausing before praising the behaviour. At other times, try commenting on how pleased you are about a particular behaviour and place the child's name last
○ when praising a group of children, you could stand by them, or walk round the room and touch them gently on the shoulder as a means of reinforcing the message
○ children can praise each other for good work and good effort, so encourage this
○ we all learn well when communication is positive and successful.

Using praise successfully

It is often helpful to link praise directly with the action. So, instead of using a general phrase such as 'Well done', say, 'Well done for putting your rubbish in the bin.' This will:

○ teach the child what the appropriate behaviours are
○ make the child feel good at doing what they have done
○ prompt the child to remember to do the right thing next time
○ remind other children to do the right thing
○ encourage children to pass praise on – it's very pleasing to hear one child turn to another and say, 'That's really good colouring'
○ increase the motivation to seek praise for doing the right thing
○ provide them with a positive role model to follow (you!).

When using praise, remember to:

○ make sure that all adults in the room are aware of all the appropriate behaviours – if the children are asked to listen, other adults in the room should listen too
○ talk honestly about your behaviour – praise yourself if you have done something well
○ relate praise to effort as well as achievement, even for mundane or trivial behaviours. The more children hear praise and encouragement, the more they are likely to use these themselves. Again, you can praise yourself, 'I tried really hard to draw a good circle and am very pleased with my work'
○ let the children know that you understand that some tasks are very difficult and that they have tried really hard, even if the outcomes were not as good as they had hoped
○ help the child to understand why the praise was delivered. Use phrases such as, 'While I was walking around I noticed you working very hard on your drawing'
○ be honest if you forgot to praise a child for something. It does not matter if you remember later in the day, or even later in the week, but make sure you pass a comment on to the child and say, 'I forgot to say so at the time, but I was really pleased with the way that you helped me tidy away on Tuesday.'

LIST 48 Getting children used to praise

Some children do not respond to praise. Their kind acts and good behaviour may have never been noticed or commented on, and some have only ever heard negative comments. Some children are constantly reminded about how often they make mistakes or do the wrong thing, and this can have a terrible effect on a child's confidence and self-esteem. When someone eventually says something nice, the child is very confused and may respond negatively. Children need to *learn* to hear nice things about themselves. So:

○ Make the child part of a group of children you are praising – this way the child does not feel singled out.
○ Comment on the work, not the child, e.g. 'That's a beautiful drawing', rather than, 'You've done a beautiful drawing.' The difference is subtle, but powerful.
○ Make the praise very private and out of earshot of other children.
○ Use facial expressions rather than words – a big smile and thumbs-up from you means that a child does not have to listen to himself being praised.
○ Use very low-level praise such as 'Thank you'.
○ Remember to praise the child who seems to be 'good all the time'.

The hard-working child

Hard-working or helpful children deserve praise as much as any other children. Without it they may become resistant to working because they feel they never get praised despite their efforts. They may notice this before their teachers do, and you may find that the child:

- ○ misbehaves in order to get your attention
- ○ stops working, or hands in poor quality work
- ○ seems very demotivated by learning tasks
- ○ interrupts frequently during lessons
- ○ starts to disrupt other children's work
- ○ does a good piece of work and spoils it
- ○ draws or scribbles on their books
- ○ draws or scribbles on someone else's books
- ○ becomes grumpy and unhelpful
- ○ complains of being ill or tired
- ○ stops doing homework
- ○ demands your attention, where previously they were very undemanding
- ○ learns quickly that bad behaviour is a sure-fire way to get noticed.

You will need to try and repair this behaviour by:

- ○ making sure the child is noticed when they are working
- ○ using praise frequently, and in both subtle and obvious forms to help the child appreciate that hard work and compliance in the classroom will be rewarded
- ○ providing the child with 'special jobs' to help them feel more positive about you
- ○ using names to remind the child of what you want them to do
- ○ smiling and giving clear signs of approval to the child
- ○ immediately praising the child for 'doing the right thing'.

LIST 50   Prompts

Using a prompt is a very positive way of helping a child to succeed. Prompts mean that you don't have to tell a child off, but they are a subtle means of reminding the child of what you want them to do. You can use indirect or direct prompts. In many cases, a child who is keen to please will respond to the indirect prompt very quickly but if this strategy is unsuccessful, a more direct prompt, a reminder, will usually work. You could try:

❍ speaking to a child next to the target child – praise this child's work or the effort they are putting in to try and complete the task
❍ commenting on how hard all the children on the table are working, without saying anything about the child who is not working
❍ providing a simple, and general, reminder about the instructions, which does not target anybody in particular
❍ giving clear reminders about how much time is left for the task
❍ reminding the children of the anticipated outcomes of the task, again without targeting a specific child.

If the child is not responding to indirect prompting:

❍ use the child's name and remind them about the task. As soon as they start working provide praise
❍ make a gentle comment about your expectations, 'I think you'll be able to manage this task'
❍ check that the child has understood what is expected. Ask him/ her to repeat the instructions to you – this way you can provide praise for being able to say what the task is. This acts as a prompt and you are able to praise the child as soon as they start work

Children who are used to receiving praise develop an internal dialogue and learn to evaluate their own work and behaviour. Then they may not need so much praise because

❍ their self-esteem is secure
❍ they are not so in need of extrinsic motivation (external sources) because they have developed an intrinsic motivation which

allows them to work hard at a task because they believe that they will feel good about themselves and the task once it is completed.

But remember, children:

- ○ always benefit from being told that they have done well when new challenges are hard and the effort they have made is recognised
- ○ sometimes feel that as they get older people forget to say, 'Well done'.

Top tip: Use simple, positive, encouraging language that leaves the child in no doubt about what good behaviour means.

Rewards

7

LIST 51   Start as you mean to go on

It is very important to reward good behaviour. You can reward behaviour you want to encourage by showing how pleased you are with it.

- ○ Praise each child every day for actions such as being friendly or helpful.
- ○ Catch children behaving well.
- ○ When children play successfully with other children, praise them for it.
- ○ Try and ignore small behaviours such as whining and minor squabbles – turn your back and walk away.
- ○ If you have worked out the ground rules, make sure that you stay out of children's play, unless they break those rules.
- ○ Speak directly and firmly to a child when correcting poor behaviour.
- ○ Try to get across that it is the behaviour that is wrong and not the child.
- ○ Think carefully before you make any threats or promises and try to be consistent – if you promise or threaten something then you must carry it out, otherwise the child will stop listening to you.
- ○ Make sure that others who care for the child use the same approaches so that they can be consistent too. It is very confusing for children if there are different rules and different approaches to correcting behaviour.
- ○ Expect to have some bad days.
- ○ When things are going well, try and remind yourself that you have done well.
- ○ Have a graded response to a child's achievements.
- ○ Remember that the children who find it most difficult to behave will need the most frequent rewards.
- ○ Remember, you can always make a restart. Both you and the child need the opportunity to start again if necessary.

LIST 52   Using rewards in the classroom

Rewards should be second nature to teachers who work with children. They should be:

- frequent
- given genuinely
- delivered in a variety of ways
- linked directly to the behaviour
- linked to effort as well as achievement
- linked to social as well as academic behaviours.

Positive role models have a positive effect on children's behaviour, so ensure that:

- all staff that work in the class with children provide high levels of praise and positive reinforcement for good behaviours
- positive behaviour is modelled in front of parents
- rewards are used frequently
- classroom successes are celebrated, privately or in front of other children.

LIST 53   Developing reward systems

Rewards encourage good behaviour and make it more likely that such behaviour will happen again. Developing them can be daunting but remember:

- encouraging words and smiles cost nothing, are easy to give and will prove very effective
- peer approval is a powerful reward
- if there is a class reward system, make sure that the rewards are available to every pupil
- rewards do not work for ever, so be prepared to change them from time to time
- make it clear exactly what you are rewarding
- when establishing a new reward or behaviour, be generous with your rewards
- state clearly the criteria for getting a reward
- praise is one of the best rewards that you can get. Be natural and vary your comments.

Simple rewards

- A smile
- Some eye contact
- Verbal praise
- Giving a few moments or minutes of quality time
- Listening to a pupil
- Showing interest in their work, life or their interests outside school
- Playing games with children
- A special reward only given out by you
- A headteacher's reward
- A merit or points systems
- Certificates
- Trophies
- A special class reward (e.g. extra free time)
- A special school reward
- Special privileges for an individual or group
- Recognition of behaviour at an assembly
- An award at presentation events
- A display of work – make sure others comment
- A special visit.

Celebrating achievements

To celebrate good behaviour and achievements:

○ ask the child to choose a stamp to put on work or the back of a hand

○ have a special sheet that the child can stamp, if they do not want to mark their work

○ have a sticker chart or smiley face chart on the wall of the classroom

○ have a daily diary or a weekly planner in which positive comments can be written

○ ask the child to write comments about their work and support this using a smiley face or sticker

○ have a jar of small sweets from which the child can select (some staff do not approve of this method of reward but children love it!)

○ let a child choose a play activity

○ choose the child to be a monitor in the class

○ ask the child to do an important job, such as holding open the door or taking the register to the office

○ ask the child to take the example of their good work to another teacher

○ have end-of-lesson 'celebration time' when good work can be positively commented on

○ ask the child to tell the others why you are so pleased with their work

○ let the child choose a picture onto which stickers can be placed to complete the scene, e.g. decorations on a Christmas tree, stars in the sky.

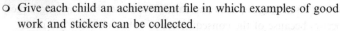

LIST 56   Positive rewards

○ Give each child an achievement file in which examples of good work and stickers can be collected.

○ Have sticker charts which, once a number of stickers have been collected, lead to a choice of reward. This must be discussed with the child in advance, as different children will choose different rewards.

○ Let the child choose the story or songs.

○ Let the child be first in a queue.

○ Allow the child to sit close to you during story time.

○ Tell the parents about the good behaviour (if possible on the same day).

○ Ensure that there are regular reports to parents which focus on the behaviour.

○ Make sure that there is a space in the child's report for plenty of positive comments.

LIST 57 The problems with punishment

When discussing rewards and sanctions, remember learning largely occurs because of the consequences of behaviour. We are more likely to do something if we are rewarded for it. Punishment has the following problems:

○ It must be applied consistently and immediately, and it depends on the exact crime committed!
○ It may lead to non-attendance to avoid the punishment, or other avoidance strategies.
○ It can be time consuming for the teacher and may even be stressful.
○ It does not teach what the pupil should do, rather what they should not do.
○ It can exalt the status of the punished.
○ It can role-model bullying.

If you must sanction. . .

If you feel you have no option other than to apply sanctions,
remember:

○ use them sparingly
○ punishments can easily be rewarding, such as playing with the
  computer outside the headteacher's room
○ constant nagging is not effective and can increase the poor
  behaviour it is supposed to change
○ nagging can put a negative focus on the child rather than the
  behaviour
○ make sure the child knows what they have to do if a similar
  situation happens
○ be as brief as possible
○ speak quietly to demonstrate that you are in control
○ give eye contact and stay close to the child
○ be fair – do not punish a whole class unless every child is at fault
○ make sure children can predict your behaviour. Do for each of
  them what you want to do for one
○ if you make a threat, see it through (unless of course you angrily
  said you'd kill them all!).

Effective sanctions

○ Ignore the behaviour – make it obvious that you are ignoring it.
○ Intervene non-verbally, e.g. by moving closer to the pupil.
○ Give a verbal reprimand, not a diatribe!
○ Use eye contact to give your view.
○ Remind the pupil in a private place.
○ Remind the pupil in a public place.
○ Take back lost time at break or during relaxed activities.
○ Use report books or cards.
○ Inform parents and discuss the behaviour with the parents with or without the pupil.
○ Send the pupil to another teacher.
○ Send the pupil to the headteacher.
○ Get a senior staff member to remove the pupil.
○ Take away points or merits – but beware, if these have been earned you risk pupils not striving to gain such merits in the future.
○ Give a job around the school.
○ Limit movement.
○ Take away a privilege – an appropriate one.
○ Disallow access to a facility, such as climbing apparatus at breaktime.
○ Ask for apology verbally or perhaps in writing.
○ Devise a contract, signed to make it 'official'.
○ Target the individual behaviour constructively.
○ Use peer pressure to help alleviate unacceptable behaviours.
○ Use some form of isolation.
○ Write the pupil's name in a poor behaviour book.
○ Exclude the pupil from their group for a short while.
○ Exclude the pupil from playtime or lunchtime.
○ Exclude the pupil from an activity during class time.

Top tip: Be consistent in all you do.

Working Together

L I S T 60   Involving all staff

It is very important that all staff work together to ensure good behaviour. Many schools have staff who are not directly teaching children, but who have regular contact with the children. These include:

- ○ the school secretary
- ○ midday supervisors
- ○ kitchen staff
- ○ parents who come in to help
- ○ the caretaker
- ○ people who deliver school meals
- ○ staff who work in before- or after-school clubs

It is vital that everyone:

- ○ is aware of the policies and principles upon which the school operates
- ○ appreciates that systems are only as strong as the weakest link
- ○ realizes that children are very quick to work out who is a 'soft touch' when it comes to rule-breaking.

LIST 61 Teaching assistants

Teaching assistants are now commonplace in the classroom. When they are in your class it is your role to manage them, although they will have their own duties to fulfil. Try to involve them as they will play an important part in ensuring good class behaviour. If you have little or no management experience, seek help from others or ask to go on a short course on managing assistants.

Involve them where possible in:

○ lesson and curriculum planning
○ understanding the purpose and aims of the lesson
○ preparing and collecting the required resources
○ deciding the role they will play in your classroom management
○ greeting pupils on entry – especially if you have a problematic class, as more children can then be settled more quickly
○ checking that pupils have the correct equipment
○ checking that homework is completed
○ using non-verbal cues to remind pupils of expected behaviours
○ reminding pupils of the class rules
○ supervising the tidying away of resources
○ seeing the pupils out to break
○ standing by the door to say goodbye to pupils at the end of the day.

Most importantly, if you ask for the attention of the class, the teaching assistant should also attend, modelling the required good behaviour. This is essential for good class behaviour. In other words, ensure that they contribute to the smooth running of your class.

LIST 62   The SENCO's role

In school the special educational needs coordinator (SENCO) has a crucial and pivotal role, especially when it comes to managing behaviour. This person takes responsibility for:

○ overseeing the day-to-day operation of the school's SEN policy
○ coordinating provision for the children with special educational needs
○ liaising with and advising fellow teachers
○ managing the learning support assistants
○ overseeing the records of all children with special educational needs
○ liaising with parents of children with special educational needs
○ contributing to the in-service training of staff
○ liaising with external agencies, including the local authority's support and educational psychology services, health and social services, and voluntary bodies.

To do this the SENCO must:

○ have a clear understanding of SEN issues
○ possess good organizational skills and high levels of knowledge in all areas of the curriculum and behaviour management
○ be a human resource manager
○ be able to manage budgets and identify areas of need
○ actively support the needs of children and staff working in the school
○ be able to work effectively with the senior management team, governors, parents and other agencies who visit school
○ be highly knowledgeable with regards to legislation, subject information, the DfES guidance and guidance from other organizations
○ write policies and reviews
○ be able to assess pupils' individual needs and prepare appropriate programmes
○ take responsibility for reviewing and monitoring progress.

LIST 63 Working with the SENCO

As the SENCO has to oversee all the programmes for the children with special educational needs, it is vital that the class teacher provides good quality information. To help the SENCO, class teachers should:

○ keep good records
○ try to identify the source of the problem and possible solutions
○ talk to other adults who work in the class to see if there are patterns of behaviour
○ make sure that difficulties have been discussed with parents
○ alert all staff to the difficulties and ask for possible ways forward
○ check with teachers who have taught the child in the past about what worked for them
○ think about what changes would help them and the child
○ ensure that they have differentiated work appropriately
○ set up a low-level monitoring system which provides the child with high levels of positive feedback
○ allow the child to take part in the target-setting process
○ keep a record of each incident to demonstrate the extent of the problem
○ review the progress and revise the targets
○ set up a clear and usable reward system for the child
○ let the child have access to a range of resources and apparatus that may help to minimise the problem, e.g. a quiet space for working, appropriate ICT and software
○ check that motor co-ordination difficulties, visual/hearing difficulties have all been considered as possible roots of the behaviour problems
○ implement a social skills/emotional literacy programme
○ think about setting up a 'buddy' or mentor system with a child from another class
○ let the child have access to an adult who does not usually work in the class but who can act as a 'friend'
○ consult with the SENCO about possible courses of action.

Supporting children with behaviour difficulties

Children who have behaviour difficulties require their own individual education plans (IEPs). At the Early Years Action and School Action stages of the Code of Practice the class teacher will already have had discussions with the child's parents about their concerns. The IEP should:

o identify the target behaviours
o put appropriate strategies into place
o contain targets which are SMART:
  - Specific
  - Measurable
  - Attainable
  - Relevant
  - Time-related
o be discussed with the child
o be supported by work in the classroom and in the whole school.

It is important that all members of staff are aware of the child's individual programme and the strategies which are to be utilized. The SENCO may wish to ensure that there are briefing sessions in which staff will be informed of such programmes.

School Action Plus

At the School Action Plus stage of the Code of Practice:

○ outside agencies may be involved with supporting the child or providing information to staff

○ additional support, from within the school's resources, may need to be allocated in order to help the child and implement strategies successfully

○ the programme will need to be discussed with parents and possibly linked to reward schemes taking place at home

○ if possible, there should be regular meetings with parents while the IEP is in place, and reviews should certainly involve parents

○ the child should have the opportunity to help with target setting

○ the IEP should include information about:
  - the short-term targets set for or by the child
  - the teaching strategies to be used
  - the provision to be put in place
  - when the plan is to be reviewed
  - success and/or exit criteria
  - outcomes (to be recorded when the IEP is reviewed)
  - information that is additional to or different from the differentiated curriculum plan

○ where a child with identified SEN is at serious risk of disaffection or exclusion, the IEP should reflect appropriate strategies to meet the child's needs

○ a pastoral support programme should not be used to replace the graduated response to special educational needs.

LIST 66

Social, emotional or behavioural difficulties (SEBD)

Children with severe behaviour difficulties are likely to be at the School Action Plus stage and will probably require considerable extra support. The Code of Practice states that a child with such difficulties may require some or all of the following:

- ❍ flexible teaching arrangements
- ❍ specialized behavioural and cognitive approaches
- ❍ rechannelling or refocusing to diminish repetitive and self-injurious behaviours
- ❍ provision of class and school systems which control or censure negative or difficult behaviour and encourage positive behaviour
- ❍ provision of a safe and supportive environment
- ❍ help with the development of social competence and emotional maturity
- ❍ counselling to adjust to school expectations and routines
- ❍ help with acquiring the skills of positive interaction with peers and adults.

Children who demonstrate features of emotional and behavioural difficulties may be:

- ❍ withdrawn
- ❍ isolated
- ❍ disruptive
- ❍ hyperactive
- ❍ lacking concentration
- ❍ presenting challenging behaviours.

The local authority, in conjunction with the school and parents, will need to consider on an individual basis whether appropriate interventions can be provided through School Action Plus or whether they need to undertake a statutory assessment.

Involving parents

Often, at parents' evenings, advice is sought as to how best parents can handle poor behaviour at home. Knowing the child well may help you to give appropriate advice. Try not to step outside your level of expertise, but you could discuss some of the following:

○ Rewards – the need for physical contact, including hugs, joint activities such as telling stories or trips to the local playground, or more concrete rewards such as small toys or magazines.

○ When to reward – as soon as possible after good behaviour, initially every time they do what is wanted, less often as they start behaving, but always praise them and tell them why they are in your 'good books'.

○ Modelling techniques – a parent could praise others in the same way they praise and encourage their own child. If necessary, demonstrate to a child the exact behaviour that is needed.

○ Don't expect too much at once – reward for trying and for each step towards the final behaviour. For young children it is often best to start with the last step, as they know this best.

○ Ignoring behaviour – this is a powerful technique, but sometimes difficult for parents to do, especially when travelling round the supermarket! Remind parents to reward the child when they do the right thing. Never ignore behaviour that is dangerous, e.g. running away or not holding a hand when crossing a road.

○ Distraction techniques – moving the child on to a different activity is often a good way of teaching and modelling good behaviour and ensuring that the child plays and works constructively.

○ Removing privileges – this can be a powerful way of improving behaviour. Favourite games or activities can be removed for a short period of time. The sooner the right or privilege is restored the sooner it can be used again as a sanction!

○ Encourage the use of rewards rather than the removal of privileges.

○ Consider putting together a short school booklet on useful tips for parents if this is a common issue – perhaps in liaison with an external agency such as the educational psychologist or behaviour support teacher.

Top tip: There are always others there to help you, so seek support and advice.

Temper and Tantrums

9

LIST 68 Learning to understand emotions

We all know that children are a product of their genes and the environment in which they are brought up. There is no doubt that the models of behaviour that children are exposed to influence the way that they behave. Children who have learned one way of behaving may not have any reference to other role models and have not had the opportunity to learn other ways of responding and behaving. Sometimes we forget this, and we also forget that behaviour is taught. A key to understanding behaviour is understanding emotions. Remember that children:

❍ may have very strong personalities virtually from the day that they are born and want to assert themselves
❍ may not like to hear the word 'no', and need to learn that there is a limit to how many needs can be met
❍ must be taught the rate at which such needs can be met and that this may change
❍ need to learn the limits of what is acceptable
❍ should hear positive language to avoid feeling angry or rejected
❍ need to learn about the main categories of emotions and link these to themselves
❍ need to understand their own anger, and yours, by hearing talk about this emotion
❍ need to realise that there are many ways of solving the same problem but they will not be able to do so if they continue to be angry
❍ can persist with inappropriate behaviour patterns if they are not taught alternative ones
❍ learn how to increase their bad behaviour to get what they want
❍ may get into big trouble in school if they cannot handle their own emotions

- may cause a great deal of upset to other children and teachers with their angry outbursts
- may spend a great deal of time outside the classroom or working on a one-to-one basis with a member of staff
- may cause other parents to complain to the school about the behaviour that their own well-behaved children are seeing
- may run the risk of exclusion.

Teachers and other adults need to:

- get to know children and respond to them in an appropriate way
- help children to learn how to handle other people and the world around them
- be aware of the triggers of the inappropriate behaviour so that preparation can be made to avoid these or find ways to work around them
- have consistent patterns of behaviour themselves so they can manage their own emotions and prevent problems from escalating
- realise that their own personality may sometimes clash with that of a child
- have the confidence to manage their own behaviour well and to help children to do the same
- have support systems within schools so that they know where to turn if a child is behaving inappropriately
- be prepared to talk to parents and find solutions to prevent recurrences.

In many cases, it is helpful if adults are prepared to:

- say how they are feeling
- focus on positive emotions
- accept that there is a wide range of emotions that adults and children experience
- help the child to acknowledge a range of feelings
- discuss how emotions may vary over time and in different situations
- show that they can control, rather than lose, their temper
- acknowledge that there are different ways of managing anger and emotions
- explain to the child what they can do to lessen the anger

○ use simple language to tell the child what they plan to do to put it right
○ be prepared to apologise, if they feel that they have shown too much anger.

Remember:

○ a child's mood does not usually last as long as an adult's
○ every child needs to learn how to interpret their emotions and those of other people
○ the more frequently a child becomes angry the more it will become a habit, and they may end up becoming a real expert in terms of intensity, timing and situation!

LIST 69   Temper tantrums

Many adults worry about children having tantrums because they are:

○ embarrassing
○ hard to manage
○ time consuming
○ a demonstration that the child is in control
○ emotional outbursts that, once triggered, can only go one way
○ likely to recur
○ likely to increase in intensity
○ likely to become more successful if they are allowed to persist
○ very deskilling if an adult cannot successfully manage the behaviour
○ likely to create very negative emotions that are hard to control for both adults and children
○ damaging to the individual who has tantrums, and they can lead to the maintenance of bad, uncontrolled behaviour throughout life
○ easy to escalate, resulting in destructive or violent behaviours
○ an obstacle to learning other ways to solve problems
○ a demonstration of immaturity
○ often difficult to repair
○ very socially isolating
○ a good way to make everyone feel bad.

Why children throw tantrums

Tantrums are a common behaviour, especially among two- to three-year-olds, and many parents report that their children have temper tantrums up to the age of six or even above. We all hope that by the time a child gets to school they will no longer be having tantrums, but some children have learnt that this is a successful way to express themselves and have not had the opportunity to learn other ways. A tantrum or emotional outburst may occur because a child:

- is thwarted by an adult
- is tired or hungry
- is frustrated
- thinks it will ensure that they get what they want
- has not learnt other ways to express him/herself
- is impatient
- has poor language skills
- has poor understanding of adult behaviour
- is unable to delay gratification
- has poor emotional literacy
- has not learnt that there are other ways to communicate effectively with adults
- is impulsive and impetuous
- does not have the skills to do something by him/herself
- cannot negotiate a successful outcome
- has a short emotional fuse
- has learnt that tantrums work
- has been resistant to strategies such as distraction or attempts to pacify
- is genuinely and appropriately cross about something and feels a very strong sense of injustice
- has been taunted, bullied or encouraged by peers to 'lose it'
- has very low self-esteem and cannot problem-solve their way out of a corner
- feels very inadequate and that no matter what they do they will not be liked by others, or be successful in their learning
- desperately wants to get out of a situation and has no other recourse than 'fight or flight'.

How to handle tantrums

In many schools, it may only be the very young children who have tantrums. As children get older, they learn how to avoid situations that will make them very cross or have learnt a range of strategies to prevent them becoming so cross that they are out of control. When a tantrum does occur it can be very difficult to manage, especially if the teacher is not prepared. Unfortunately, most of us do not get the opportunity to 'practise' what to do if a child has a tantrum, so teachers need to think carefully, before the situation arrives, about how they will manage a very cross child.

To handle a tantrum successfully you have to:

○ be prepared for it
○ think calmly and clearly
○ be aware of your own safety, and that of other children
○ not try to make sense of the senseless behaviour
○ detach yourself from any personal outbursts the child may direct at you
○ be determined, well organised, decisive and ready to take action
○ be in control of your own emotions and ready to use your emotional intelligence to the full
○ have a strategy ready that you feel you can comfortably adopt, depending on:
  – the age of the child
  – your mood and tolerance level
  – where you are
  – who else is around
  – pressures of time
  – the level to which you have practised your skills
○ remember that if the tantrum is rewarded it will be repeated and the child will use this strategy more often and more successfully
○ make sure that your behaviour does not 'add fuel to the fire'
○ know what you will do when a tantrum is over.

LIST 72 Strategies for managing angry behaviour

To be most successful in managing angry behaviour you should be able to:

- ○ ignore where you are and who else is around
- ○ feel secure about your own skills
- ○ moderate your response according to the intensity of the angry behaviour
- ○ control your own emotions and bring very simple strategies into operation in order to ensure success.

Strategies to try

- ○ Use selective ignoring – a tantrum is only useful to the child if it is played out in the company of the significant audience. If no one is watching or paying attention there is little point having the tantrum.
- ○ Use distraction – an alternate activity can be very helpful, particularly if it is possible to make this activity look very interesting. If the child wants to become involved, they may forget the fact that they are feeling cross.
- ○ Use simple, calm language, and give a running commentary.
- ○ Try to gauge whether the behaviour is real anger or if it is an act for your benefit.
- ○ Give the impression that you are not shocked or scared by the behaviour.
- ○ Make sure that other children know that you are still in charge – even if you do not feel that this is the case.
- ○ Move away from the child who is cross.
- ○ Give attention to another child in a calm and positive manner – the child may temporarily increase the intensity of the tantrum in order to try and regain your attention, but if you maintain your calm the child will probably give up and come and take part in a new activity.
- ○ Remind the child who is having a tantrum of what they are supposed to do.
- ○ Insist, in a very calm voice that you would like the child to settle down and do what you have asked.

- Remind them that you can see that they are angry and that you can help them to solve the problem.
- Ensure that other children are safe and that they are not at risk from the child's behaviour.
- Remember the school's policies for positive behaviour strategies and sanctions.

LIST 73   Dealing with flaring tempers

If you are in a situation where the child becomes very cross:

○ remind them of what they are supposed to be doing
○ deliver instructions in a calm, clear, concise way, which leaves the child in no doubt about what it is expected
○ use positive language – negative language can remind the child of what it is they are not supposed to be doing, and then they will go and perform this action. If a child is having a tantrum and we say, 'Don't kick the table', the chances are that he will go over and kick the table. If we remind him that, 'When you are calm, we can...' then there is a clear message about how he should behave.
○ make sure that another child is sent to get help if you feel it will be needed
○ move the other children away so they cannot be damaged or hurt by the behaviour
○ if necessary, send all the children out of the class, having sent one of them to inform another teacher
○ keep your body language calm
○ inform the child very clearly of what you are going to do and why, 'I'm going to sit down so that I can finish marking these books'
○ allow the child to make a new start when they 'get it right'
○ don't hold a grudge or remind the child about their behaviour in a very negative way. This will make them very unhappy and can damage self-esteem
○ consider having a quiet word about the inappropriate behaviour later – phrase this in a positive way, and remind the child that they managed to overcome their anger and demonstrate an appropriate calm emotion so that they could be re-introduced to the activity and regain positive adult attention
○ make sure parents and other staff are consulted about the behaviour
○ remember the emotional literacy development programmes. A child who has a very quick temper should immediately be referred for one of these or take part in a school programme to help develop emotional awareness
○ sit down and think calmly when you have the opportunity, to see if you can work out what caused the behaviour and if there are ways of avoiding this in the future.

Using time out

If low-level strategies do not work, you may need to remove the child from the situation for a brief while. This is called 'time out'. Remember, this is not a punishment that means that a child should be excluded from the situation for a long period of time. It is:

○ assertive
○ definite
○ time-limited.

Have a place that you can take the child to, then:

○ use clear, specific language about what they are expected to do while they are there
○ walk away
○ count for very brief time (allow one minute for each year of the child's age)
○ invite the child to return to the activity and use appropriate behaviour in that situation. In this way, the child has been temporarily excluded.

If you have a child who is interested in regaining your attention, they will want to get back to being with you and their friends, rather than be isolated. This strategy can be very effective in the classroom, but remember:

○ use it selectively. If it is used too harshly or too often it can have a detrimental effect on a child's self-esteem and their behaviour may become worse
○ give the child the opportunity to 'put it right' by doing the right thing – remaining in the time-out situation for a brief period of time is a way of 'putting it right'
○ once you have asked the child to return to the activity, they need to know that they have done the right thing
○ they may find it difficult to rejoin the class or the group so you need to make sure that there is very little fuss when the child returns
○ praise the appropriate behaviour.

In many cases teachers use a 'naughty chair' or 'naughty corner' but this can have negative connotations. You might want to call it the 'thinking chair' or the 'remembering chair'. This removal should ensure that the child is facing away from other children, but is within earshot.

LIST 75 Tantrums in older children

Tantrums in older children can be rather ugly. We do not expect an older child to have a tantrum, as they should have learnt how to control their anger and know that a temper tantrum is a rather 'babyish' way of behaving. But it does happen, so be prepared.

○ Use the same principles of management for younger children in Lists 71, 72 and 73.
○ Try to identify the triggers which may lead to a temper tantrum and act quickly by:
  – moving the child
  – removing other children
  – defusing the situation.
○ Help the child to realize that the behaviour is unacceptable and will not be tolerated in the classroom.
○ Remind the child how to behave.
○ Speak in a calm, clear, decisive voice to a child who is becoming angry.
○ Tell the child exactly what to do.
○ If you feel confident enough, stand close to the child and talk in a calm voice.
○ Use the 'broken record method', saying the same reassuring thing over and over again.
○ Use 'I' statements rather than 'you' statements as these can help to defuse the situation.
○ If necessary, remove the child from the situation without handling them or causing further distress and use the time-out strategies described in List 74.
○ Send a reliable child to get help.
○ Be mindful of your own safety.
○ Discuss the behaviour later in a calm and quiet way so as not to trigger another angry outburst.
○ Don't show anger yourself – if you do so, the child may be unable to control a further outburst and this will make them feel stupid in front of their friends.

LIST 76 Stop tantrums becoming a habit

Angry behaviour can be very powerful. It can help children to get what they want or stop things from happening that they do not want to happen. Children can very quickly learn that adults are uncomfortable with, and do not know how to handle, tantrums. They are also aware that the bad behaviour may be rewarded (e.g. they may be sent out of the class and not have to complete their work).

- ○ It may be that a child who finds it difficult to control their behaviour with one teacher manages their behaviour perfectly well with another. If you can study that teacher's particular methods and strategies, the difficult behaviour can be avoided for other teachers.
- ○ Point out that other children do not have tantrums – this can help to establish the idea that different ways of responding are better.
- ○ Spend some time with the child, watching other children to see how they learn and how they behave when they are trying to manage difficult situations.
- ○ Discuss ways of seeing a situation differently – it is often the interpretation of a situation that causes the angry reaction.
- ○ Discuss alternative ways of solving the problem.
- ○ Try to notice and become aware of situations which may trigger the angry behaviour. Make sure you notice, and praise, the behaviour if the child manages to control their temper.
- ○ Use immediate and delayed praise to remind the child of the situation where they did not act in an angry manner, even though they may have had just cause to do so.
- ○ Provide good role models in school – for those children who may not have had role models teaching them a better way to respond, this can be a very good way of helping a child to become more emotionally literate.
- ○ Remember to reinforce the child's behaviour through emotional literacy programmes in the classroom, making sure that these pervade the whole curriculum.
- ○ Make sure you try and change your responses to the child.
- ○ Seek specialist advice if the child's behaviour continues to be very angry.

○ Contact the local authority which will have teams dedicated to supporting children with such behaviour difficulties. Referral to an educational psychologist may also be helpful.

Controlling emotions

When you are dealing with an angry person you may feel angry yourself and you may even feel humiliated. You will almost certainly feel unable to cope and deskilled as a teacher. These feelings are normal. However, do not let them cloud your judgment, and if you have made a mistake, admit it.

If children have a problem with anger or aggression:

○ encourage them to use a simple strategy to enable them to manage in difficult situations. Suggest:
  − walking away from the situation
  − counting to ten before taking any action
  − thinking about the consequences of actions before taking them
  − breathing slowly when cross – this is worth practising
  − finding a teacher or designated person to tell immediately
  − ignoring the event or situation and not worrying about it
  − going and playing with a best friend
  − running around the playground, or any other strategy that takes them away from the situation
○ remind them of a phrase or 'mantra' which you have previously discussed using
○ role-play a situation with the pupils to help them develop a strategy to cope in difficult situations
○ make sure all incidents are recorded so that in extreme cases further help can be obtained from support agencies
○ objectively record the facts, not your emotional responses.

Exorcising your anger and aggression

Use this for yourself, your pupils or your colleagues.

○ Tense your muscles and breathe in.
○ Stay tense for five seconds.
○ Now begin to relax, starting with your head and moving slowly down your feet – breathing out slowly as you do this.
○ Repeat the above several times.
○ Once you can do this, think of someone who has made you angry or something that has frustrated you.
○ Tense up, focus on your anger or frustration.
○ Relax as indicated above.
○ As you relax, feel the anger draining out of you.
○ Feel the emotion leaking out of the tips of your toes and visualize it as a puddle at your feet.
○ Once you have drained your anger, step away from the puddle and leave your anger behind.

Top tip: Always be calm and professional.

Bullying | 10

LIST 79 — What is bullying?

Children learn most effectively in schools where they and staff feel safe, secure and happy. This means we must all treat each other with kindness and respect. Bullying is where a child or a group of children exercise some kind of control over another against their will. All bullying behaviour has three things in common:

- it is deliberate and hurtful
- it is repeated a number of times (one-off situations are not usually regarded as bullying)
- it is difficult for those being bullied to defend themselves.

Bullying may involve:

- physical behaviour – hitting, kicking or stealing possessions
- verbal behaviour – name-calling, insults, racist remarks or even threats
- more indirect behaviour – such as spreading true or untrue stories about the victim or excluding them from groups.

LIST 80   Types of bullying

- Pushing, shoving, punching, kicking, poking
- Severe physical assault
- Abusive telephone calls – especially vicious when texted on a mobile phone
- Physical harassment or the infliction of pain
- Interference with a desk or even a pencil case
- Personal property defaced, broken, stolen or hidden
- Demands for money in or out of school
- Aggressive body language
- The 'look'
- Nasty notes – these can be frightening
- Sending to 'Coventry' or any other place for that matter
- Name-calling – fatty, prossie, paki, baldy, teacher's pet, four eyes. . .
- Personal remarks about appearance or personal hygiene
- Verbal abuse, threats to people's families, etc.
- Damage to clothing or school books.

Make sure *you* as a teacher do not bully by using:

- sarcasm
- humiliating methods
- degrading exercises
- intimidating gestures.

Understanding the behaviour of bullies

Children might bully because they:

○ may live with people who abuse them in some way
○ may have learnt that aggression and violence are effective
○ believe dominating others is the best means to get their own way
○ live in a household which is harsh and where physical punishment is common
○ live for part of their life in an environment which is highly inconsistent in terms of its rewards and punishments
○ have faced sudden emotional outbursts
○ have not been taught it is wrong
○ are encouraged to bully by friends
○ believe it is just a 'bit of fun'
○ believe this is how one socializes
○ are going through a difficult time at home or school
○ are copying behaviour they have seen
○ have been a victim of bullying
○ have a strong wish to dominate others
○ have found their size and strength or even age are useful ways of achieving goals.

L I S T 82   Bullies and victims

Pupils regularly need to be made aware that bullying will not be tolerated in school. All staff should be vigilant, especially when on duty around the school.

Bullies:

○ are often popular and have a 'following' of children who like to be seen to be in the core group
○ rarely bully on their own if part of a group, preferring the presence of the main bully to enhance their confidence
○ place a lot of importance on power and status
○ regularly tell lies to get out of trouble
○ often blame others and show little remorse for their actions.

Victims:

○ are often passive loners who are targeted as they readily respond and have few self-defence skills
○ tend not to be able to retaliate quickly verbally and are particularly sensitive to the comments of others. They may have weak language skills which makes it more difficult to ignore or in any way deflect comment
○ may have special vulnerabilities, such as sensitivity about their lifestyle or family, the clothes they wear or their physical attributes
○ occasionally retaliate with little chance of 'winning'.

LIST 83

Research into bullying

Research indicates that the three most helpful factors in preventing bullying or helping pupils to deal with bullies are:

○ friendships
○ avoidance strategies
○ learning to 'stand up for yourself'.

Reporting bullying is associated with several risks. Children tend to fear that:

○ their confidentiality is likely to be breached
○ nothing will be done
○ they will not be protected from the future actions of bullies
○ their parents might not believe them or might over-react and make matters worse
○ their parents might worry too much.

Important sources of help include:

○ parents – for emotional support and advice, and for raising concerns about bullying with teachers
○ confidential services, such as counselling services and voluntary organizations working with children and young people. Such organizations enable pupils to express their feelings, consider the options available to them, and have some control over the pace of disclosure, should they decide to tell a teacher or parent about bullying.

(Based on a report called *Tackling Bullying* by Christine Oliver and Mano Candappa, Thomas Coram Research Unit, Institute of Education, 2003.)

LIST 84 Taking action

If you think that a child is distressed because they are being bullied you must act quickly to avoid further damage to self-esteem or to their physical and mental well-being.

❍ Read and follow the school policy on bullying.
❍ Know the school code on behaviour and discipline and enforce it.
❍ Keep your eyes open for possible bullying.
❍ Always act as a good role model.
❍ Develop good self-esteem in the bully and the victim.
❍ Listen carefully to the victim and the bully.
❍ Record incidents accurately.
❍ Check out facts where you can.
❍ Try not to blame young people.
❍ Make it clear that the behaviour is unacceptable.
❍ Discuss the general issue of how to behave with your class.
❍ Get the victim and the bully to record the incident if they are old enough – this helps to demonstrate its seriousness.
❍ Tell pupils to report any bullying or harassment and act on the information immediately.
❍ Stress the horrendous nature of such behaviour to all.
❍ Stop bullies from joining a group while they persist in their behaviour.
❍ Teach them how to behave appropriately.
❍ Help victims to be less vulnerable to name-calling, and not to retaliate when bullied – remind them that others are called names as well and point out that most of the taunts are not true or valid ones.
❍ Try to build self-esteem by talking about strengths rather than weaknesses.

Some anti-bullying strategies

Tackling bullying in school is essential and it is important that activities take place throughout the school which reduce the possibility of bullying and help pupils to find more acceptable ways of interacting with each other. The following activities and strategies could be helpful:

○ Set up social skills training sessions for more vulnerable children, especially those with language difficulties, those lacking verbal skills, or pupils on the autistic spectrum.
○ Give bullies the chance of making restitution (see the George Robinson and Barbara Maines *No Blame Approach* published by Lucky Duck Publishing).
○ Teach children what to do in situations where their peers are being bullied.
○ Teach pupils at risk of bullying how to avoid getting into situations likely to promote bullying.
○ Teach pupils at risk of bullying how to deal with certain situations such as name-calling, and how to leave a threatening situation.
○ Reframe the behaviour of the bully by getting them to take on a position of responsibility and help them to see the benefits of positive rather than negative behaviour towards others.
○ Use peer-support schemes to help reduce the amount of bullying in your school. Children will need to be trained as peer supporters to help create a safe and supportive environment. Different schools have adopted different schemes. Sometimes a professional counsellor is involved in the training, or an educational psychologist. Pupils are taught listening, coping and negotiating skills. They are taught to recognize issues that they can deal with, and those that need passing on to another person.

Top tip: Be alert to potential small events that inform you about children's reactions.

Special Problems | 11

LIST 86   Attention deficit hyperactivity disorder (ADHD)

Attention deficit hyperactivity disorder (ADHD) is a medical diagnosis. Such children:

- are easily distracted
- have extreme difficulty in starting or finishing their work
- find it difficult to sustain attention
- may appear to be unusually disorganised and forgetful for their age.

If the child is also hyperactive he/she may demonstrate high levels of fidgeting, have a greater tendency to run around and is often over-talkative. All of this can lead to marked behavioural problems in the classroom. You may receive advice from external agencies, but you should also ask your SENCO for advice and support. You can help by considering the following:

- Be as consistent as possible and develop routines which are consistently implemented.
- Consider where the child should sit. Choose a position where stimulation is reduced (e.g. not looking out of a window) and try to ensure that a good role model is nearby.
- Try to avoid unpredictable transitions, such as suddenly deciding that the class will work outside.
- Encourage the child to seek assistance.
- Simplify complex directions and be as clear, succinct and concise as possible.
- Praise and reward with high frequency.
- Avoid repetitive tasks – try and break tasks down into short, achievable parts.
- Consider having a daily notebook for the child who can then monitor his/her progress and achievements.

- Make sure any homework instructions are written down.
- Encourage a 'buddy' system so that help is immediately available.
- Give only one task at a time and always ensure that they have enough time to complete it.
- Be vigilant – make sure the child does not struggle with the task.
- If they are proving disruptive at the beginning of a lesson, send them on an errand, but be ready for them when they return.
- Give them feedback on their behaviour, be very constructive and ensure that they appreciate the consequences of particular actions.
- Always interact calmly and quietly. You may well need to consider a variety of other changes to your working routines and patterns, including alternative recording techniques.
- Remember, children with ADHD will need special management and special rewards and more time will be needed.

LIST 87   Autism and Asperger's syndrome

You may have children in your class who have autism or Asperger's syndrome. This is a spectrum of behaviours and some children have very mild characteristics which may make them appear as if they are deaf or have a language difficulty. Often children with autism or Asperger's will have been identified, and you will have been given appropriate support and training. However, sometimes there are children who have not been diagnosed, and you need to be aware of some of the characteristic behaviours. Such children may:

- have difficulty with social interaction, social communication and social imagination
- sometimes have great difficulty in interpreting body language, gestures and facial expressions
- demonstrate literal understanding of everyday expressions
- appear to be devoid of appropriate facial expressions
- use inappropriate eye contact, either by avoiding eye contact, or looking too long into someone's eyes as they are talking
- have a very strong need for structure and routines and without these, become very anxious and agitated
- have some difficulties with physical movement and the coordination of fine motor skills
- show strong preferences for certain activities
- prefer to have things in a fixed way and find it very difficult to deviate from this pattern of behaviour
- be over sensitive to auditory or visual stimulation
- have some obsessive routines
- find it difficult to make friends because they cannot understand the rules of the games other children are playing and, if there are rules, may believe that they should be fixed
- be rather solitary, but enjoy physical activities such as running and climbing.

Managing autism and Asperger's syndrome

Many children with autism and Asperger's syndrome can function successfully within the mainstream classroom if their condition is fairly mild. You will need to seek support from specialists with the local authority, who will have knowledge about the effect of these conditions. It is helpful to remember that the behaviour may be very distinct from other children's but is not intended to be aloof or rude, it is simply that their understanding of social rules and situations may be very different from other children's. However, there are some simple guidelines which are very helpful.

○ Remember that high levels of structure and routine help to minimise anxiety and agitation.

○ Pre-empt any unexpected changes that may happen by giving plenty of warning and reminders.

○ Provide children with a quiet and calm working environment.

○ Try not to raise your voice or have loud music in the class as this can cause agitation.

○ Do not overload the child with sensory information – children may prefer to work in a situation which has few visual distractions. Keeping auditory distractions to a minimum can also be helpful.

○ Use visual or verbal timetables to promote an understanding of the daily routine.

○ Make sure that you give the child the opportunity to respond.

○ Teach social rules in a highly explicit way and practise them regularly.

○ Make sure that all staff know that the child may find playtimes difficult.

○ Have very good links with parents, so that you can find out about events at home and any anxieties or upsets that may have occurred.

○ Encourage social interaction through the use of board games, turn-taking activities and responsibilities for a certain task within the class.

○ Be alert to the difficulties with social interaction – use a buddy system but make sure the buddy has been told how to help the child with autism.

LIST 89 Dyspraxia

Another difficulty that primary school teachers are aware of but often do not fully understand is dyspraxia (also known as developmental coordination disorder). Many young children who have difficulties in the classroom are often later identified as having dyspraxia. You may need to watch out for these problems as, in combination, they can make a child very unhappy and may lead to misbehaviour in the classroom. Common indicators include:

- Tendency to fidget a lot.
- High levels of excitability, with a loud/shrill voice.
- Easily distressed and prone to temper tantrums.
- Constantly bumps into objects and falls over.
- Lacks any sense of danger (jumping from heights, etc).
- Continued messy eating – may have problems coordinating a knife and fork and may prefer to eat with the fingers. Frequently spills drinks.
- Avoids construction toys such as jigsaws or building blocks.
- Poor fine motor skills – difficulty in writing, drawing or using scissors.
- Lack of imaginative and creative play.
- Seems isolated within the peer group and finds it hard to form relationships with other children. Rejected by peers, some children may prefer adult company.
- Limited response to verbal instructions – may be slow to respond and have problems with comprehension.
- Inability to remember more than two or three instructions at once.
- Limited concentration – tasks are often left unfinished.
- Poor listening skills.
- Always leaning or lying on the table when working.
- Difficulty in adapting to a structured school routine.
- Difficulties in PE lessons.
- Slow at dressing and unable to tie shoelaces or fasten buttons.
- Barely legible handwriting.
- Immature drawing and copying skills.
- Immature use of language.
- Slow completion of class work.
- Hand flapping or clapping when excited.

- Sleeping difficulties, including wakefulness at night and nightmares.
- Reporting of physical symptoms, such as migraine, headaches or feeling sick.

Children who have difficulties like these may soon notice the difference between themselves and other children. It's not surprising that children who are slow writers, poor at drawing, struggle with sport, have problems remembering information and expressing themselves get upset and start to misbehave! Consult your SENCO as to how to minimize their problems in the context of your school.

LIST 90 Drugs alert

Drug abuse in primary schools is a growing problem, especially in some areas. Be aware of local problems and make sure you know your school policies. Look out for the following behaviour changes in a pupil or group and report them so that a fuller picture can be obtained:

- ○ Sudden and unexpected changes of mood
- ○ Irritability
- ○ Unusual aggressive behaviour
- ○ Loss of appetite
- ○ Loss of interest in previously followed activities
- ○ Extreme tiredness
- ○ The formation of a new and different group of friends
- ○ Secretive behaviour
- ○ Odd stains, smells or marks on the body or on clothes.
- ○ The telling of lies
- ○ Drowsiness in a normally lively person
- ○ Physical changes, such as loss of weight
- ○ Changes in attendance or punctuality.

These are not definite signs of drug use, so do not jump to conclusions but seek help and support as quickly as possible.

Avoiding problems on school trips

Problematic behaviour can often ruin what should be a really good school trip, but there are some steps you can take to make sure things run as smoothly as possible. It's also vital that you check your school policy on trips, consult your local authority and read the latest government guidelines before you leave.

○ Prepare a procedure for what to do if a pupil gets lost or separated from the main group and explain it to the children.

○ Pair the pupil with another one (friends if possible) – emphasize the responsibility for looking out for each other.

○ Explain sanctions for bringing the school into disrepute and give examples of unacceptable behaviour.

○ Print out some guidelines of how to enjoy a trip rather than a list of what not to do.

○ Discuss what pupils should do if they discover personal facts about others in the class or about a member of staff. Get pupils to think of some examples and how they would react. Role-play potential situations but handle this sensitively.

○ Get pupils to list their possessions and ask them to check periodically against this list, e.g. at the end or beginning of each day.

○ Ensure that information divulged on individual consent forms is kept confidential, and reassure parents that this is the case. More information is likely to be given by parents if they feel that confidentiality will not be breached. Staff have to ensure that a child's health and welfare is not discussed within hearing distance of others. Enquire about allergies, food sensitivities, phobias, medical regimes, etc.

○ Set some time aside, perhaps after the evening meal, for pupils to seek individual advice, e.g. about home sickness, having no friends, personal problems, an accident – this is applicable to boys as well as girls.

○ Handle personal student information sensitively. A few young people suffer from enuresis (bedwetting). Parents do not always notify staff of this as students worry that they won't be allowed to go or that other children will laugh at them. Dyspraxia and emotional problems can be possible causes of enuresis. Children with emotional difficulties due to family circumstances may also suffer from it.

Top tip: Know any syndromes or specific difficulties your children have and make sure you understand what your responsibilities are.

Emotional Literacy | 12

National policy

Much research has recently centred on what makes people happy and successful. There is a train of thought that says this is not due to cognitive intelligence but to emotional intelligence. Many examples are cited of people who are not particularly clever but who have done incredibly well and are very successful in their lives. Indeed, we can all think of people who may not be particularly well educated, who have not got many qualifications, and who do not have particularly good jobs, but they are very happy and seem to lead fulfilled lives. These may be the people who are most emotionally literate, and, because they are aware of their own feelings and those of others, they are very successful.

Schools are working on ways to improve children's emotional literacy. There are many ways to do this and many programmes on the market. Schools that use such programmes have been very encouraged by the results.

The idea of developing emotional literacy fits in well with the DfES guidance, *Developing children's social, emotional and behavioural skills: a whole-curriculum approach* (DfES 0759-2003G) which is part of the response to try and improve behaviour in schools. It:

○ emphasizes the fundamental importance of emotional literacy
○ believes this underlies almost every aspect of school, home and community life
○ believes children need to be educated within an environment supportive to emotional health and to well-being.

It aims to provide children with the skills to be effective and successful learners and to:

○ make and sustain friendships

- deal with and resolve conflict effectively and fairly
- solve problems with others all by themselves
- manage strong feelings, such as frustration, anger and anxiety
- recover from setbacks and assist in the face of difficulties
- work and play cooperatively
- compete fairly and win and lose with dignity, showing respect for competitors
- be able to celebrate the success of all children
- make a contribution towards addressing self-esteem and emotional health issues with the classroom
- be able to contribute successfully to the community
- develop an inner locus of control and be responsible for their own actions and reactions.

LIST 93 Emotional literacy programmes

The Healthy Schools initiative and the Every Child Matters agenda are trying to improve the prospects for many children across the country. There is concern that many children are growing up in difficult circumstances and are not aware of their own potential. Emotional literacy programmes link very neatly with the national initiatives that are designed to help children have happier and healthier futures. Many programmes are being introduced as part of the school curriculum. The aims are to:

○ establish a school climate, articulating specific themes, expectations, character elements, and/or values
○ build a caring, supporting and challenging classroom and school climate to ensure effective, emotional literacy teaching and learning
○ integrate and coordinate social-emotional learning programmes and activities within the regular academic curriculum and life of the classroom and school
○ increase explicit instruction in social-emotional learning, life skills and social competencies, developing a common language and positive social-emotional culture
○ increase explicit instruction in health promotion, problem prevention and problem-solving skills
○ set up systems to enhance coping skills and social support for transitions, crises, and resolving conflicts
○ provide high-quality, genuine, reflective service opportunities for pupils and staff
○ foster enduring and pervasive social-emotional effects through collaboration between home, school and community.

(Based on *The Educator's Guide to Emotional Intelligence and Academic Achievement: Social-Emotional Learning in the Classroom* by M J Elias and H Arnold, Corwin Press 2006.)

LIST 94 Emotional intelligence

For children to behave well they have to have an understanding of their own feelings and those of others. They need to develop respect for themselves and an understanding of how bad behaviour builds up negative emotions towards them. We call this emotional intelligence, and it:

○ is different from intellectual intelligence
○ encompasses self-awareness, impulse control, persistence, zeal, motivation, empathy and social deftness
○ means that a child has developed an inner locus of control (lack of emotional literacy means that a child has an outer 'locus of control' and may blame other people for what happens to them)
○ helps children to take responsibility for their actions and their consequences
○ allows a child to ask for help when things are tough
○ helps children to succeed in life.

(Based on information from *Emotional Intelligence* by Daniel Goleman.)

LIST 95   Using emotional literacy programmes successfully

Children learn behaviour and need good role models. As school is an environment where children are exposed to many role models, we need to make sure that everyone has an understanding of what good behaviour is and how best to teach it. Because of this it is necessary to ensure that:

○ everyone is aware of the chosen emotional literacy programme
○ everyone believes in the programme
○ everyone is prepared to practise to make the programme successful
○ everyone is mindful of their own behaviour in the classroom
○ everyone has the opportunity to practise those behaviours that allow them to behave in an emotionally literate manner
○ people are supported in a positive way, so they can change their own behaviour
○ the management systems promote and support all attempts at helping individuals to develop their own emotional literacy
○ everyone is honest about situations which they find difficult to manage
○ the entire school community is part of the programme – including the midday supervisors, the caretaker and parent helpers
○ celebrations are held to reward and reinforce emotionally literate behaviours
○ children are asked to take an active role in recording or preparing visual displays that celebrate the school's achievements
○ there is the opportunity to enrol outside support, if teachers feel that this would keep the children motivated and interested in the programme
○ systems are in place that allow children to realize that it is not simply academic achievements that get rewards
○ there is a focus on making the whole school a community where everyone cares for each other and is mindful of everyone else's needs
○ there is an acceptance that sometimes things go wrong, but these can easily be put right and everyone can make progress.

LIST 96   Helping to make children aware of their emotions

Circle time is a way of supporting children, improving behaviour and enhancing self-esteem. Personal and social education development is central to the National Curriculum. Circle time is a good way to:

❍ provide a safe and secure environment in which children can work
❍ explore feelings
❍ discuss conflicts in a non-blame and non-punitive way
❍ apply what has been learnt to the classroom and the playground
❍ link the social and emotional work to targets in the National Curriculum
❍ give each child an opportunity to speak
❍ let each child know that they will be listened to
❍ get to know more about children's strengths, feelings and preferences
❍ remove the feeling of competition and replace this with an atmosphere of empathy and mutual assistance.

It can help children to:

❍ feel valued and valuable
❍ believe in themselves
❍ take risks
❍ discover things they did not know about their peers
❍ learn other ways of relating to other children
❍ develop a better understanding of other children and their feelings
❍ develop an awareness of mutual support
❍ learn how to co-operate and develop an understanding of friendship
❍ build up an understanding of problem-solving and a repertoire of solutions
❍ develop a sense of wanting to belong rather than being isolated from the group
❍ respond to good models of behaviour
❍ learn the rules of behaviour
❍ take control and responsibility for their own behaviour.

Good reasons to use circle time

Circle time in itself is a planned and well-prepared activity which allows a child, through fun activities, to develop an understanding of themselves and the world around them. It also encourages children to:

○ listen to what is going on
○ learn not to interrupt
○ anticipate fun activities
○ work in pairs
○ talk a lot, but appropriately
○ have access to a 'buddy'
○ understand the expectations of circle time
○ receive prompts to encourage appropriate behaviours
○ earn rewards for appropriate behaviours
○ learn how to make appropriate choices
○ learn to be creative and use lateral problem-solving techniques
○ develop a capacity to ignore minor disruptions
○ reduce the amount of negative attention
○ receive incentives for completing activities as asked
○ be part of the planning
○ gain responsibilities and take on 'special jobs'
○ respect confidentiality
○ learn how to make mistakes without feeling bad
○ discuss difficult topics without feeling threatened and having to resort to 'fight or flight' type responses.

For more information on circle time, try some of these resources:

○ *Best-Ever Circle Time Activities* by Ellen Booth Church, Scholastic (2004).
○ *Quality Circle Time* by Jenny Mosley, LDA (1998).
○ *The Giant Encyclopedia of Circle Time and Group Activities* ed. Kathy Charner, Gryphon House (1996).

The Golden Time system

The 'Golden Time' system is used in many schools. It allows a very positive approach to be used, and involves the children as partners in their own learning.

- ○ There is a clear structure so that the teacher and children know what is expected.
- ○ It is viewed as a celebration for keeping the rules, and the children know exactly how it will operate.
- ○ There is an exciting opportunity that children will really want to participate in.
- ○ Children know what happens if they break a golden rule.
- ○ Children have the opportunity to earn back golden time.
- ○ A sand timer is used to measure lost golden time, but children are aware of the activities that they are missing, while they are waiting.
- ○ Activities are kept exciting by regularly reviewing and replacing activities and games with new, more desirable ones.
- ○ Children have a say in which activities take place during golden time.
- ○ Golden time runs alongside day-to-day activities, with encouragement, incentive and praise strategies.
- ○ Children are regularly thanked for working or behaving well.
- ○ Commendations and stickers are given out during and at the end of lessons.
- ○ Teachers are encouraged to give children physical signs (a smile, a thumbs-up) to show the children they are doing well.
- ○ Good work is explained and shown to the rest of the class.
- ○ Notes are sent home for parents, commending a child's work or achievement of a tiny target of good behaviour.
- ○ Certificates are used widely to celebrate achievement.
- ○ Responsibility and badges are linked to particular duties as rewards.

For more information on Golden Time see *Better Behaviour through Golden Time* by Jenny Mosley and Helen Sonnett, LDA (2005).

More powerful approaches

Some children need a more targeted approach to help them improve their behaviour. This is because:

○ thinking and emotional responses are interconnected
○ the feeling part of the brain is more primitive than the thinking part – it is designed to help survival through rapid responses
○ the feelings may open the 'fight or flight' pathways
○ the way that we feel about something influences our behaviour
○ feelings come first and then we act depending on our response to our feelings
○ some behaviour problems arise through maladaptive thinking
○ feeling bad feelings and thinking bad thoughts can lead to bad behaviour
○ irrational thinking may mean that we see the world or interpret events wrongly
○ we may concentrate so much on the feelings that we forget to do the thinking
○ children who can't think around a problem may behave inappropriately.

Access to a trained worker in these cognitive–behavioural methods can have positive and enduring results. Training and practice of the techniques can help children build emotional resilience and provide them with skills that they can take with them through their lives.

You may want to talk to your school's educational psychologist about these approaches. Some useful resources include:

○ *Feeling Good: The New Mood Therapy* by David Burns, Avon Books (1999).
○ *Cognitive Therapy and the Emotional Disorders* by Aaron Beck, Penguin Books Ltd (1991).
○ *Cognitive Behavioural Therapy for Dummies* by Rob Wilson and Rhena Branch, John Wiley & Sons Ltd (2005).

LIST 100 Changing how we feel

Our ways of feeling and thinking are not fixed. If a child goes to school believing that the teacher does not like him, this may alter his behaviour and he may behave in a way which prevents the teacher from liking him or his behaviour. If children are encouraged to develop rational ways of thinking about themselves and their problems then the behaviour can become more appropriate.

Intervention can be designed to identify how a problem is seen or felt and to find the right solution. It should:

○ challenge the distorted or irrational thinking
○ find different ways of thinking about the problem
○ generate a range of alternative thoughts
○ change the beliefs that have been created
○ create ways to move from the particular to the general
○ promote reasoning, rather than guessing about what might happen
○ focus on the positive aspects
○ maximise achievements
○ promote positive thinking
○ help children to accept less than perfection in themselves and their performance
○ help children to develop an understanding about themselves and the world
○ prevent personalization of events
○ identify the relationship between thoughts, feelings and behaviours
○ reduce impulsive behaviour
○ increase verbal self-instruction and appropriate responses
○ allow a redefinition of the problem
○ generate a range of solutions
○ generate and apply coping statements for changing incorrect behaviours
○ use self-reinforcement techniques for appropriate behaviours.

These methods are very powerful and can help a child to develop mature ways of thinking about a problem, the solution to the problem and to develop emotionally and socially.

119

LIST 101 Top-tip summary

- Keep up to date with national initiatives as these will affect your school's policies and practice.
- Never criticize the person, only the behaviour.
- Really work on your school and class rules.
- Remember to consider the whole child, as behaviour may reflect external influences.
- Remember to act quickly and give choice and take-up time – essential for avoiding and dealing with any trouble.
- Use simple, positive, encouraging language that leaves the child in no doubt about what good behaviour means.
- Be consistent in all you do.
- There are always others there to help you, so seek support and advice.
- Always be calm and professional.
- Be alert to potential small events that inform you about children's reactions.
- Know any syndromes or specific difficulties your children have and make sure you understand what your responsibilities are.